Raising Black Students'
ACHIEVEMENT
Through Culturally Responsive Teaching

SUSTAINABLE
FORESTRY
INITIATIVE

Certified Fiber Sourcing

www.sfiprogram.org

Raising Black Students'
ACHIEVEMENT
Through Culturally Responsive Teaching

Johnnie McKinley

ASCD

Alexandria, Virginia

1703 N. Beauregard St. • Alexandria, VA 22311-1714 USA
Phone: 800-933-2723 or 703-578-9600 • Fax: 703-575-5400
Web site: www.ascd.org • E-mail: member@ascd.org
Author guidelines: www.ascd.org/write

Gene R. Carter, *Executive Director;* Judy Zimny, *Chief Program Development Officer;* Nancy Modrak, *Publisher;* Scott Willis, *Director, Book Acquisitions & Development;* Genny Ostertag, *Acquisitions Editor;* Julie Houtz, *Director, Book Editing & Production;* Ernesto Yermoli, *Editor;* Judy Connelly, *Senior Graphic Designer;* Mike Kalyan, *Production Manager;* Marlene Hochberg, *Typesetter;* Kyle Steichen, *Production Specialist*

PAPERBACK ISBN: 978-1-4166-1059-5   ASCD product #110004   n11/10
Also available as an e-book (see Books in Print for the ISBNs).

Quantity discounts for the paperback edition only: 10–49 copies, 10%; 50+ copies, 15%; for 1,000 or more copies, call 800-933-2723, ext. 5634, or 703-575-5634. For desk copies: member@ascd.org.

Library of Congress Cataloging-in-Publication Data

McKinley, Johnnie.
  Raising black students' achievement through culturally responsive teaching / Johnnie McKinley.
    p. cm.
  Includes bibliographical references and index.
  ISBN 978-1-4166-1059-5 (pbk. : alk. paper) 1. African Americans—Education—Washington (State)—Seattle—Case studies. 2. Academic achievement—Washington (State)—Seattle—Case studies. 3. Seattle Public Schools—Case studies. 4. Cultural awareness—Washington (State)—Seattle—Case studies. I. Title.
  LC2803.S43M35 2010
  371.829'9607309797—dc22

                     2010025032

20 19 18 17 16 15 14 13 12 11 10   1 2 3 4 5 6 7 8 9 10 11 12

Raising Black Students'
ACHIEVEMENT
Through Culturally Responsive Teaching

Acknowledgments vii

Foreword. ix

Introduction 1

Chapter 1: Setting and Maintaining Clear Expectations for Content Mastery 15

Chapter 2: Student-Teacher Social Interactions 35

Chapter 3: Classroom Climate 45

Chapter 4: Classroom Management 55

Chapter 5: Curriculum and Instructional Design 69

Chapter 6: Classroom-Based Assessment. 77

Chapter 7: Cultural Competence. 86

Chapter 8: Cultural Congruence in Instruction 96

Chapter 9: Cooperative Group Instruction 113

Chapter 10: Procedures for Rehearsal, Processing, and Transfer of Learning. 121

Afterword 129

Appendix A: Assessment of Effective and Culturally Responsive Strategies (AECRS) Form 131

Appendix B: Walkthrough Feedback Forms 143

References 205

Index. 209

About the Author 214

Acknowledgments

I would like to thank the friends and colleagues whose generous and invaluable support made this book possible. The encouragement and support of my sons, Jonathan and Joseph, and my friends Alice Drummer, Dionna Pellum, and Nashonne Watkins, will always be appreciated.

I would also like to express my gratitude and indebtedness to the teachers and principals who opened their schools and classrooms to me and contributed their time, enthusiasm, and wisdom to our understanding of effective and culturally responsive teaching and learning. Though the teachers, principals, and schools are given pseudonyms within the text of the book, I would like to thank them here by name:

Schools

African American Academy
Aki Kurose Middle School
Asa Mercer Middle School
Bagley Elementary School
Broadview Thompson School
Denny Middle School
Eckstein Middle School
Fairmount Park Elementary School
Gatewood Elementary School
Graham Hill Elementary School

Greenwood Elementary School
Hamilton Middle School
Highland Park Elementary School
John Muir Elementary School
Roxhill Elementary School
Sanislo Elementary School
Schmitz Park Elementary School
TOPS @ Seward Elementary School
Whitman Middle School

Teachers

Andrew Bean

Susan Broder

Peggy Elenbaas

Alice Ellis

Beverly Ferguson

Wendy Forselius

Brian Gaynor

Beth Haavik

Jennifer Hancock

Aaron Hennings

Donald Hill

Dan Jurgensen

David Lee

Jeff Mackenzie

Barbara Mann

Eric Mansfield

John Paloy

Sally Raichle

Donna Rodenberg

Sara Roraback

Keisha Scarlett

Teresa Spiz

Sara Stipes

Sara Strunk

Marianne Trangen

Bjorn Unneland

Japhy Whalen

Janet Wilson

Melinda Woodbury

Larry Young

Principals and Assistant Principals

Terry Acena

Barbara Bahner

Dan Barton

Bi Hoa Caldwell

Lynn Caldwell

Carmen Chan

Sue Kleitsch

Marcia Knudson

Carol Lake

Birgit McShane

Ruth Medsker

Richard Mellish

Davy Muth

Eric Nelson

Cynthia Rodriguez

Antoinette Sabarots

Clara Scott

Teri Skjei

Karma Torklep

Medgar Wells

Foreword

In this book, Johnnie McKinley reveals the depth of her caring about black students' learning and describes the beliefs and values that exceptional teachers and their students follow as they grow and learn together. By sharing educators' stories, Johnnie introduces readers to classrooms where learning is continuous, where teachers and students respect each other, and where principals and teachers alike approach teaching students of color from a position of efficacy and confidence. Readers are sure to be entertained, fascinated, and enlightened by the insights they gain from these teachers' stories. They will also learn how to set and maintain expectations; establish positive social interactions; and design, implement, and assess culturally responsive teaching strategies that bring about high-quality learning.

School environments today are characterized by increasing diversity of languages among incoming students, conflict over beliefs about what students should be required to learn, and considerable divergence in thinking about the very importance of schools. It has never been more critical that students learn to think well, to understand information, to develop effective skills for using information to solve complex problems, and to communicate ideas. The strategies illustrated in *Raising Black Students' Achievement through Culturally Responsive Teaching* will help teachers achieve these important goals and, thereby, reduce learning gaps between black and white students.

Daisy Arredondo Rucinski
Professor, University of Alabama
Spring 2010

Introduction

Black kids are outspoken, so I spend lots of "closet time" with them one-on-one. I do not put kids in the hall. I spend time with them at lunchtime and offer pep talks. I figure out something they do well and commend them regularly. As a black person, I have an advantage. I share problems black people have if they don't get their behavior together. We talk about relation-ships at home, family, and friends. What I find is that if you care, then kids will perform for you. They meet me one-half or three-quarters of the way. My relationship with them is something they are looking for.
—Carla Storey, middle school teacher

This is a book about the thinking, planning, and decision making behind the practices of 31 teachers and 20 principals in the Seattle Public School District who have managed to narrow the achievement gap between their white and black students. I spent 20 months surveying, interviewing, and observing these educators, whom I call the Proving the Possible (PTP) educators. They believe in their capacity to improve outcomes for all their students and use the instructional, management, and assessment strategies discussed in this book to design instructional practices, create classroom contexts that support learn-ing, and prepare students to excel on high-stakes standardized assessments.

Despite their commonalities, in no way do the PTP educators present a monolithic view of teaching and learning. The following comments capture the complex and inextricable relationships among their philosophies, beliefs, self-perceptions about their efficacy in their professional roles, and classroom decision-making processes:

- *Adrianne Driscoll, elementary school teacher:* "Better, stronger, faster, smarter—that's one of the little mantras I share with my students. I expect them to be that before they leave me, and I say to myself that I'm the one to get them there."
- *Alex La Chuisa, middle school principal:* "It's about relationships. I tell all my teachers that one of the most important things is to connect and bond with kids."
- *Michael Wagner, middle school teacher:* "In developing relationships with my students, I try to establish that I really believe in them. I think that it is worth the effort and the time to keep planting those seeds of "I believe in you and I believe you can do it." Being personally reflective, driven to connect with students, and flexible enough to make changes to meet the needs of individual kids—those have been the most successful strategies I have used."

The PTP educators used reflective decision-making and knowledge gained from research on culturally responsive teaching strategies to improve their students' achievement. Researchers such as Pasch, Sparks-Langer, Gardner, Starko, and Moody (1991) and Irvine and Armento (2001) have conducted comprehensive studies that demonstrate that culturally responsive approaches dramatically improve the academic performance of low-income and minority students. Additionally, researchers such as Boozer, Krueger, and Wolkon (1992); Cook and Evans (2000); Haycock

(1998); and Sanders and Rivers (1998) suggest that achievement gaps are mainly due to the following five root causes:

1. Negative teacher expectations, attitudes, and beliefs;
2. Disparate treatment and opportunities to learn;
3. Poor interpersonal relationships;
4. Negative student identity and lack of motivation; and
5. Inadequate instructional responses to cultural backgrounds and learning styles.

In addition, PTP educators grounded their teaching strategies in the following five factors that researchers have found are key to closing achievement gaps (Banks et al., 2000; Cole, 1995; Irvine & Armento, 2001; Ladson-Billings, 1994, 1995, 2000; Pasch et al., 1991; Shade, Kelly, & Oberg, 1997; Wang & Walberg, 1991; Zeichner, 1996):

1. Constructive teacher attitudes and beliefs that nurture student motivation;
2. Positive interpersonal relationships that draw on the social constructivist aspects of teaching;
3. Social activist approaches that address racism, social injustices, and disparate expectations, conditions, and opportunities to learn;
4. Establishment of a cultural context for learning based on students' backgrounds; and
5. Effective and culturally responsive instruction and assessment.

Given the complex nature of teaching and learning, educators must address the root causes of achievement gaps interdependently and simultaneously. The PTP educators acknowledged that their work required a great investment of time and effort. Middle school teacher Susan Lansing confided, "I'm just trying to be an effective teacher for all kids. I think I'm spending 60 to 70 hours a week at this because I enjoy it. I like doing what I do!" These educators' stories confirm that we can approach teaching students of color from a position of efficacy, confident in what we and our students can achieve.

In addition to revealing the thinking, planning, and decision-making processes of effective educators, this book will take readers on virtual walkthroughs of five PTP classrooms to observe how the teachers implemented their successful strategies. Readers will also find a classroom and school assessment survey in Appendix A that outlines procedures for focusing discussions, planning, and observing effective teaching strategies in the following ten categories:

1. Setting and maintaining clear expectations for content mastery
2. Student-teacher social interactions
3. Classroom climate
4. Classroom management
5. Curriculum and instructional design
6. Classroom-based assessment of student learning
7. Cultural competence
8. Cultural congruence in instruction
9. Cooperative group instruction
10. Procedures for rehearsal, processing, and transfer of learning

Pause for a minute to recall students whose academic lives differed from one another's due to such factors as race, ethnicity, privilege, or physical ability. Think, too, about instances when students performed better than expected given their demographic traits. During the walkthroughs in this book, you will see how the PTP teachers differentiated learning contexts, instructional approaches, and classroom-based assessments in response to their students' culture, race, gender, and class.

Achievement Gap Statistics

McWhorter (1997) has asserted that "forty years after the Civil Rights Act . . . [and] affirmative actions . . . African American[s] still perform lower than any major racial or ethnic group in the [United States], at all ages, in all subjects, regardless of class" (p. 2). Over 10 years later, educators continue to find achievement gaps among students of comparable ability and grade level on such measures as the Scholastic Aptitude Test (SAT), the National Assessment of Educational Progress (NAEP), and the Programme for International Student Assessment (PISA); grade point averages; and high school and college enrollment and dropout rates (Cook & Evans, 2000; Gonzales, Cauce, Friedman, & Mason, 1996; Herrnstein & Murray, 1994; Simmons, 1999; Singham, 1998; Spradlin, Welsh, & Hinson, 2000). Recent reports by Katy Haycock (2008), executive director of the Education Trust, a nonprofit dedicated to improving student achievement, show a mix of converging and widening gaps; for instance, although the gap between white and black and Latino nine-year-olds was narrowed on 2004 NAEP reading scores, scores still showed wider gaps between these groups than in 1990.

Furthermore, the science, reading, and mathematics PISA scores of U.S. 15-year-olds show that the fourth largest gaps are between students of high and low socioeconomic status (with the latter group comprising primarily students of color). The importance of effective pedagogical responses for students of color is especially important given the increasing racial and ethnic diversity of the U.S. population (Gallego, Cole, and the Laboratory of Comparative Human Cognition, 2001).

Demographics of the PTP Educators

Many researchers attribute achievement gaps to demographic and cultural disparities between teachers and students, and to teachers' low expectations for poor and black students (Grant & Secada, 1990, cited in Gallego et al.; Nieto, Young, Tran, & Pang, 1994, cited in Freel, 1998; Noguera & Akom, 2000; Toch, 1998). Thus, when I present the results of my research on PTP educators at regional, national, and international conferences, audiences invariably inquire about the demographics of the PTP teachers. I usually begin by explaining that Seattle Public Schools is an ethnically and economically diverse urban district of over 47,500 students, 100 schools, and 2,175 elementary and middle school teachers. In the two years that I studied the district, blacks made up 23 percent of the student population at the 20 PTP schools. The district as whole serves students from over 70 countries, speaking 129 languages—parent/student participation letters are provided in Cambodian, Chinese, English, French, Laotian,

Spanish, Tagalog, and Vietnamese. Seattle Public Schools is also economically diverse: while 41 percent of the students in the 20 PTP schools received free or reduced lunch, rates from school to school ranged from 16 to 83 percent, with 12 of the 20 schools reporting rates above 50 percent. For the sake of comparison, consider that the average U.S. school serves neighborhoods where 15.7 percent of households live in poverty (National Center for Education Statistics, 2007a).

The ethnic makeup of PTP teachers mirrored that of teachers in the state of Washington and in the United States as a whole. Over 83 percent of the nation's teachers are white, as are over 90 percent of teachers, paraeducators, and school administrators in Washington State (National Center for Education Statistics, 2007b; State of Washington, Office of the Superintendent of Public Instruction, 2008). At the time of my research, 14 percent of the PTP teachers and principals were black, 10 percent were Asian/Pacific Islanders, 2 percent were Latino, and 74 percent were white. As in the rest of the country, PTP educators were predominantly female. Of the 51 educators participating fully in the study from February 2002 through October 2003, 67 percent were female. 61 percent of the participants were teachers, and 39 percent were principals. Over 86 percent of the PTP educators reported having over 3 years of experience, with some having more than 10 years' experience. Twenty percent had worked in 1 to 4 schools, and 11 percent in 5 to 12 schools. Sixty-three percent had worked with students from diverse backgrounds for over 3 years, with some having more than 10 years' experience. Many of the educators had had extensive experience with both high- and low-performing students in such urban centers as New York and Chicago. The diversity of experience among PTP educators ensured that each brought a unique perspective to his or her duties.

How the Study Was Conducted

To determine which teachers were most effective at narrowing or closing the achievement gap between white students and students of color, I focused on data from two standardized state assessments in reading, writing, and mathematics: the 2001 Washington Assessment of Student Learning (WASL) and the 2001 Iowa Test of Basic Skills (ITBS).

First, I conducted a quantitative analysis of data on the 47,450 district students in 3rd to 8th grade classrooms that showed no gap between black and white students' average Normal Curve Equivalent (NCE) scores on the 2001 ITBS (for grades 3, 5, and 8) or between the number of black and white students scoring 400 on the 2001 WASL (for grades 4 and 7). To ensure the presence of a pattern, I only studied classrooms with five or more black and white students who met either of the WASL and ITBS benchmarks.

Second, I matched the identified high-performing students to their classroom teachers (in elementary grades) or language arts and mathematics teachers (in secondary grades) and school principals. The 31 teachers and 20 principals who ultimately consented to participate in the study represented outliers among teachers in the district for their effectiveness teaching black students. Some PTP teachers maintained that they became stronger teachers after being chosen for the study, and began to reflect individually and with colleagues on their classroom practices. The principal at a school with two such teachers noted that they had improved considerably since the completion of the study.

The findings of the PTP study suggest that teacher efficacy is not dictated by teachers' backgrounds, but rather by a confidence in their effectiveness, self and peer reflection, professional development, collaboration, and coaching to adapt strategies to meet students' needs and backgrounds.

The TCRC™ Model

It is virtually impossible to create and sustain . . . conditions for productive learning for students when they do not exist for teachers.

—Seymour B. Sarason

The Teaming for Culturally Responsive Classrooms (TCRC) model encompasses two important components that promote student achievement: professional development and improved instructional practices. The professional development component encourages both individual reflection and group inquiry into practices observed during instructional walkthroughs. The instructional component focuses on learning and using culturally responsive strategies suitable for all disciplines and grades and for any curriculum. Kati Haycock (2008) found that teachers in high-performing schools regularly observe other teachers, have time to plan and work collaboratively, take on many other leadership tasks at the school, and provide new teachers with generous and careful support and acculturation. The TCRC model promotes each of these actions. As they progress collaboratively through the six phases of the model, educators will, over time, become expert in the use of effective and culturally responsive strategies—able to explain the theory and principles behind each strategy, demonstrate the strategy in action, and help other teachers sustain use of the strategy in the classroom.

Teamwork and the TCRC Model

Teamwork is a key element of the TCRC model. Creating a social environment that allows reflection on and sharing of professional practices is vital to the process of implementing culturally responsive teaching and learning strategies. As Pasch and colleagues note, teacher performance improves through self- and peer-reflection, and student performance improves when teachers adjust their practices in response to student needs, contexts, and culture (1991).

The PTP principals reported that the teachers in their schools spent a great deal of time reflecting on and analyzing their practice, and indicated that they aided teacher reflection by actively encouraging and monitoring their use of new strategies. An unexpected finding in the study was that PTP teachers credited powerful teaching teams and collegial

and personal relationships—teaching team partners, mentors, spouses, and friends—with providing coaching that strengthened their practice and their beliefs that students could meet their high expectations.

It is important for discussions of teaching and learning among educators to be structured; otherwise, feedback on implementing new strategies might be too vague to be of any use. In the TCRC model, teachers in a school are organized into teams of three to six for the purpose of providing support to one another while pursuing the common goal of incorporating effective and culturally responsive strategies in their schools. These teams can be easily formed regardless of a school's organizational structure or fiscal resources and have worked successfully in both elementary and secondary schools.

Change Processes and the TCRC Model

Being part of a school system in no way guarantees a comprehensive understanding of how schools work. According to Sarason, initiating change in schools first requires us to understand how power is used in planning and implementing change and how the effects of power relationships percolate throughout a school system (1990). Thus, in the Explore phase of the TCRC model, instructional coaches facilitate staff discussions on how to understand and participate authentically in the decision-making processes behind the implementation of new strategies. It is equally important for educators to collaborate with administrators and teachers' unions when developing structures and tools such as walkthroughs, to ensure that they are not used for evaluating teachers and do not violate the law. When attempting to establish new strategies as integral components of their organization's culture, educators might consider the conclusions drawn by sociologist Everett Rogers in his research on professionals in multiple disciplines (1995). Rogers found that members of a group use a process called "diffusion" to attain a group-wide understanding of innovative practices or ideas. In the Share phase of the TCRC model, educators share effective new instructional strategies with each other until a critical mass is reached and the strategies are widely implemented. At the same time, educators also share the changes that they expect to see in student and teacher interactions after using the new strategies, as well as changes observed in student engagement and achievement. This type of focused examination of professional progress in achieving goals has helped scores of schools move from a culture of isolation to one of collaboration and support (Ziegler, 2006).

The Phases of the TCRC Model

The TCRC model includes the following six phases based on categories developed by the North Central Regional Educational Laboratory (NCREL) for the national Strategic Teaching and Reading Project (NCREL, 1994), which was certified in 1992 by the U.S. Department of Education's Program Effectiveness Panel:

1. **Explore** by building a knowledge base
2. **Compare** by observing models and examples
3. **Compare** by reflecting on your own practice
4. **Compare** by listening to student voices
5. **Develop** by changing your practice
6. **Share** expertise

When implementing the TCRC model, educators work as teams to progress through each of the model's six phases. The activities listed here will help you develop your abilities to explain the principles and theory behind a strategy, demonstrate the strategy in action, and help other teachers sustain the strategy's use in the classroom. Activities for each phase can be repeated with each new strategy adopted. Continue until all your chosen strategies are learned, internalized, implemented, and routinely embedded in daily teaching procedures.

Phase 1: Explore by Building a Knowledge Base

- Members of a grade-level or content-area team of teachers and administrators individually complete the AECRS form in Appendix A.
- The team convenes to discuss and analyze the members' responses on their forms.
- Based on the frequency scores from the form and the professional judgment of team members, the team members list the strategies for the category they have selected on the form in order of priority.
- Individual team members write down their definitions of each strategy in the category using their own words. They then

pair up to discuss both the definition and their prior knowledge of the category with a colleague.

• Team members work together to generate a list of the indicators, norms, techniques, procedures, and behaviors associated with the chosen category's strategies.

• A coach leads the team in a discussion on the decision-making processes behind choosing and implementing strategies in schools.

Phase 2: Compare by Observing Models and Examples

Educators

• Observe a discussion among colleagues who feel competent in using the chosen strategies.

• Watch as colleagues demonstrate the chosen strategies in action during lessons. (Alternatively, educators may watch a video demonstration.)

• Plan and conduct classroom walk-throughs.

• Invite colleagues to model a strategy in their classrooms.

• Examine existing lesson plans to determine whether they employ the chosen strategies.

• Review lesson plans that employ the chosen strategies, noting their content and contexts.

• Assess how frequently and how well teacher volunteers or master teachers in video demonstrations have implemented the chosen strategies in the classroom.

• Discuss their observations of chosen strategies in action.

• Engage in a facilitated discussion of the indicators shown in demonstration lessons, which the team members then list.

Phase 3: Compare by Reflecting on Your Own Practice

Educators complete the following steps individually:

• Analyze student work to determine their students' strengths and needs

• Self-assess their use of strategies and choose new ones they would like to include in their own teaching

• Establish goals for setting, reviewing, and revising performance

• Conduct research on the techniques, procedures, and behaviors associated with the chosen strategies

In the team, educators

• Brainstorm ways to adapt (or alternatives to) examples of strategies from their research that they think would work in the school.

• Analyze the content and context of lesson plans (and of any attendant strategies) for their upcoming lessons.

• Identify strategies that teachers are using successfully in the school, that are within their control or influence, and that they estimate will be the most successful at addressing areas of concern.

• Discuss focus areas for subsequent lessons and team meet-ups.

Phase 4: Compare by Listening to Student Voices

Educators
• Interview students in classrooms where teachers use one or more of the chosen strategies, asking them how often the strategies are used in class, how the strategies affect their learning, and what they believe the purpose of the strategies is.
• Ask students to show how they demonstrate their learning in class.
• Debrief the interviews.

Phase 5: Develop by Changing Your Practice

• Educators identify problems they encounter when using the chosen strategies in class.
• The team as a whole agrees on changes that should be made to lessons, student assessments, and classroom environments.
• Individually, educators rewrite or modify textbook lessons to align with the chosen strategies.
• Team members discuss the ways in which they revised their lessons to align with the chosen strategies.

Phase 6: Share Expertise

Educators
• Develop a schedule for conducting classroom walkthroughs or collecting relevant student work to further analyze chosen strategies.
• Describe the teacher and student behaviors that they expect to observe once the chosen strategies are implemented, based on data collected during walkthroughs and through analysis of student work.
• Develop a method for providing feedback to each other on the strategies and contextual features observed during walkthroughs.
• Continuously assess the school's capacity to develop plans for using new strategies.
• Identify a team member who can coach a colleague in the early stages of using a chosen strategy.
• Model the use of chosen strategies in a colleague's classroom.
• Exchange lesson plans with colleagues in different content areas to determine whether strategies are usable across the board.
• Publicize progress on action plans to implement chosen strategies.

The TCRC Walkthrough Protocol

Instructional walkthroughs, which have become widely used in schools within the last five years, are at the heart of the TCRC model. There are two general types of walkthroughs: internal, which are conducted by teachers within the school, and external, which are conducted by visiting teachers from other schools. Walkthroughs allow staff to learn from each other while taking an honest, purposeful look at the type and quality of classroom instruction in their schools (Davidson-Taylor, 2000, as cited in Ziegler,

2006). Although walkthroughs alone may not improve student performance, studies suggest that they result in greater teacher efficacy and student achievement (Frase, 1998, as cited in Ziegler, 2006).

Successful walkthroughs don't just happen; they need to be carefully planned, conducted, and analyzed. In the following sections, we'll examine what should happen before, during, and after an instructional walkthrough.

Selecting a Focus Area

Prior to conducting walkthroughs, teachers in a content-area or grade-level team compare the strategies that they currently use with culturally responsive strategies that have been proven effective and commit to developing their observational skills. A list of effective strategies can be found on the Assessment of Effective Culturally Responsive Strategies (AECRS) form in Appendix A. Working on one category of strategies at a time, the educators conduct research, analyze lessons and student work, observe exemplary classrooms, engage in individual reflection and group inquiry, apply professional judgment based on school priorities and needs, and complete instructional audits such as the AECRS form to narrow their focus on up to three of the 10 categories of strategies.

When completing the AECRS forms, teachers first select one or more categories of strategies on which to focus, based on the perceived needs of their school. They then individually rate how frequently they use each strategy within those categories on a scale of 1 to 10, with 10 being "very frequently" and 1 being "very rarely." Next, they add up these individual tallies and calculate a group average for each strategy. Here are the ratings that the teachers at one PTP school came up with for strategies in the classroom-based assessment category:

- *Strategy:* Align instruction and curriculum content to authentic assessment methods. *Rating:* 7.27
- *Strategy:* Align assessments to the content, format and complexity, and level of difficulty of teaching and learning activities. *Rating:* 5.5
- *Strategy:* Use frequent and continuous assessments to determine skills and knowledge, provide feedback on goals, and create interventions. *Rating:* 6.18
- *Strategy:* Make decisions using multiple samples of students' best efforts toward standards, consistently scored against public criteria. *Rating:* 5.18
- *Strategy:* Use culturally sensitive, fair, and unbiased assessments of cognitive and social skills. *Rating:* 4.72
- *Strategy:* Augment standardized tests with a variety of assessment strategies appropriate to diverse learners, including observations, oral exams, performances, and other CBAs. *Rating:* 8.27
- *Strategy:* Teach students how to assess and monitor their own development of skills, knowledge, and dispositions. *Rating:* 8.09
- *Strategy:* Match assessment to students' language and home culture. *Rating:* 7.36
- *Strategy:* Use culturally sensitive, fair, and unbiased assessments of cognitive and social skills. *Rating:* 7.73

- *Strategy:* Ensure that language abilities and special needs do not interfere with demonstration of competence by providing coaching, accommodations, interpretation, and translation support as needed. *Rating:* 6.45
- *Strategy:* Vary content, times, and format of assessment sessions in response to students' energy and engagement patterns. *Rating:* 7.18

Based on these data and their discussions, the teachers decided that a walkthrough would be conducted in the class of a colleague who was able to successfully align his classroom-based assessments with large-scale assessments, as this was the strategy that they used least frequently.

Forming and Training Walkthrough Teams

Once the grade-level or content-area team has selected a focus area, team members break up into smaller teams to conduct the walkthroughs, with team members each receiving a copy of the walkthrough feedback form for the chosen focus area (see Appendix B). In addition to the individual copies, each team should also have a group copy of the form. For the purpose of external walkthroughs, walkthrough teams should be made up of three to five educators, with each serving as host of a walkthrough by external observers during the school year. If a school initiates an internal walkthrough, teachers should be organized into two groups: walkthrough teams and host teachers. It is best for teachers to volunteer to host walkthroughs; principals should not

mandate which teachers play host (Ziegler, 2006). During preliminary meetings prior to the day of the walkthrough, teams should be trained in walkthrough protocol—that is, the etiquette, roles, and tasks of the walkthrough—by someone knowledgeable about the walkthrough process; such training will make the short discussions in pre-observation meetings flow smoothly. Teams should create a list of the specifics of the walkthrough protocol, make copies of the list for all team members, and bring the copies with them to the walkthrough. If teams will also be interviewing students as part of the walkthrough process, they should also develop a protocol sheet enumerating permissible topics of discussion and examples of interview questions to pose to students during the training sessions.

Pre-Observation Preparation Meeting (30 minutes)

On the morning of the walkthrough, teachers who have volunteered to be observed meet briefly (5–10 minutes) with their principal to discuss the walkthrough process. (If the observers are visiting from another school, the host school's instructional leadership team uses this time to welcome them and offer them refreshments.) The principal then meets with the walkthrough teams, welcoming them to the school if they are external and answering any questions the teams may have about the focus area to be observed. Then, a trained facilitator is assigned to each team.

Members of the walkthrough teams decide on the roles each of them will play during the walkthrough and on what aspect of classroom interactions they will make notes. For example, one member of each observation team might take responsibility for making a quick sketch of the room and noting important features of the physical environment, while someone else might be responsible for tallying strategies observed on the feedback form. Different team members should also be selected to make note of teacher or student activities related to relevant strategies on the first page of the form, while another group of team members notes specific examples of the evidence related to the strategies. Finally, one team member should be assigned to make note of instructional strategies that were expected but not observed.

Conducting Walkthroughs (30 Minutes)

A facilitator leads each walkthrough team on visits to three classrooms, spending a maximum of 10 minutes in each. Teachers should do their best to ignore the observers and proceed with their lessons. If introductions are conducted, they should take less than a minute. The teachers should be aware of what the teams will be looking for and understand that the walkthroughs are not evaluations; the teams are there simply to observe and take notes. After each walkthrough, the facilitator leads the team out of the classroom and on to the next room or to the debriefing area.

Student Interview Walkthrough

Observation teams can learn valuable information about the processes and outcomes of instruction and student learning by conducting interviews with students during walkthroughs. With the cooperation of the teachers being observed, teams can schedule when students will be interviewed to discuss learning activities, processes, work samples, and instructional outcomes using interview protocols developed during their preliminary trainings. When students reveal the ways in which they are demonstrating their learning, educators are able to deepen and reflect on their understanding, allowing them to more accurately discern how different strategies are implemented in the classroom.

Interviewers should spend a maximum of 10 minutes with each student in a classroom, working from a prescribed list of questions related to their focus area. They begin by introducing themselves to the students and explaining the purpose of the interview questions. During the interviews, the interviewers record student answers to questions and ask them to share work samples or portfolios related to the focus area. When the interview is over, the interviewers thank the students for their participation. In the debriefing, interviewers share the students' responses and discuss the work samples with the students' teachers. It is helpful for teachers to bring samples of student work for close examination during these discussions. Teachers reflect on the student responses and work to develop generalizations about students' strengths and weaknesses, from which they can go on to develop instructional strategies, lesson plans, and classroom-based assessments based on interpretations of student responses and work samples.

First Classroom Debrief (30 Minutes)

At this point, the facilitator for each team, who has been trained in walkthrough protocols and reflective questioning, involves the observers in a discussion about the evidence they gathered on their feedback forms. Reflecting on the focus question helps educators become self-directed learners and managers of their work (Costa & Garmston, 1994). In keeping with many union policies and codes of professional conduct, observers are not to evaluate the quality of the teaching they observed. During the debriefing, a recorder lists the evidence gathered in the walkthrough along with questions that the observers ask on the group feedback form. (Note that the individual and group forms are formatted identically.)

Next, the facilitator asks the observers to generate feedback for the observed teachers in the form of reflective questions. These questions should be aimed at helping the school and teachers think deeply about teaching and learning, without being judgmental (e.g., "How will you know you have successfully engaged all students?") (Ziegler, 2006).

End-of-Day Debriefing (45 Minutes)

At the end of the day, the walkthrough teams reconvene in the meeting room, along with the principal and the team facilitators. Each participant relates his or her observations, providing feedback related to the focus question in the form of specific evidence gathered and reflective questions. Here are some possible reflective questions to ask in the debriefing:

• What do the strategies observed say about the classrooms in which they were used?
• What are teachers and instructional leaders doing to develop a common

understanding of strategies that address differences in culture, socioeconomic class, race, ethnicity, learning styles, language, and prior experiences? How might coaches and instructional leaders support teachers as they address these differences?
• What have we learned that we can act on immediately?

The team as a whole then summarizes the evidence, looks for patterns, and notes which expectations were and weren't met. Then, the team identifies the most useful reflective questions to help the school and teachers improve teaching and learning. The principal notes the observers' suggestions, comments briefly on the feedback, and collects each team's group feedback form. The principal collects all the group feedback forms and plans how to get the feedback to the teachers. If the observers are external, educators from the same school should get together at this point and discuss how best to share what they learned with their home school. The full group then plans the next steps to take. Here are a few suggestions:

• Write a thank-you note to each observed teacher, recognizing at least one effective practice noted during the walkthrough.
• Provide feedback to observed teachers in any of the following ways:
  - Note general patterns of interaction and student learning activities observed in all classrooms.
  - Share specific examples (without identifying the teacher or classroom) of strategies observed.

- Share a reflective question regarding professional practice for the observed teachers to consider.
- Verbally share specific, positive examples of effective teaching strategies observed in a particular classroom with the teacher in that classroom.
• Learn more about the instructional, contextual, or assessment strategies by
    - Conducting study groups.
    - Watching videotaped lessons of exemplary teachers.
    - Forming teams to observe colleagues using targeted strategies.
    - Enlisting the help of teaching peers who will videotape colleagues using targeted strategies.
    - Examining student work.
    - Conducting a lesson study.

• Revisit individual classrooms to more deeply understand a specific instructional practice or a potential area of development for the observed teacher.

*   *   *

The remainder of this book will explore 10 themes that capture how the PTP educators' efforts helped close achievement gaps by addressing equity and expectations, contextual features and classroom environment, instructional planning, assessment of student learning, and instruction. Though the names of the PTP educators quoted have been changed, the comments are taken directly from in-depth interviews that I conducted with them over the course of my study.

1

Setting and Maintaining Clear Expectations for Content Mastery

In this chapter, we will examine how the PTP educators implemented the following strategies:

Category: Belief in Self-Efficacy

Strategies: Teachers . . .
- Believe in their capacity to make a difference in student learning.
- Strengthen skills, knowledge, and self-efficacy through professional learning.

Category: Role and Mastery Expectations

Strategies: Teachers . . .
- Hold high academic and personal expectations for every child.
- Hold students to established state and district standards.
- Set objectives and provide regular feedback on accomplishment.
- Regularly remind students that they are expected to learn.
- Ensure that students understand their individual roles in content mastery and task completion.

Category: Equitable Access to Resources and Opportunities to Learn

Strategies: Teachers . . .
- Provide students with equitable access to learning opportunities regardless of academic gaps or needs.

• Provide resources to meet the needs of all children regardless of academic gaps or needs.

Category: Fostering Student Self-Efficacy and Responsibility
Strategies: Teachers . . .
• Believe in and promote student self-efficacy, individual ability to achieve, and positive self-regard.
• Scaffold and gradually transfer learning responsibility to students, teaching them to self-monitor skills development.
• Provide developmentally appropriate choices and decisions about alternative assignments to reach academic goals.
• Foster students' abilities to persevere on learning tasks.
• Regularly remind students that learning will be challenging and rigorous.
• Provide instruction and extensive modeling on how to strategize in the face of difficulty.
• Reinforce student effort and recognize accomplishments.

Belief in Self-Efficacy

Like other effective and culturally responsive educators, the PTP teachers were driven by a firm belief in their ability to make a difference in their students' learning regardless of their racial or cultural backgrounds, which led them to set and maintain high and clear expectations for themselves and their students. As elementary teacher Diana Granger explained, "You can mouth the words 'All children can learn,' but unless you really believe it and put it into practice, it's not going to happen."

To support their students' belief in their own abilities, PTP educators scaffolded and gradually transferred learning responsibility to them and helped them learn how to support and monitor their own and their peers' progress. The educators made sure that students understood their roles in mastering content, completing tasks, and meeting academic standards. Principal Alicia Baldwin made the following observation about teachers at her school: "There's a commonality with all these teachers. They look at their own data; *they* want to do well, and they truly do want *their kids* to do well."

Expectations, Motivation, and Academic Achievement among Students of Color

Gallego, Cole, and the Laboratory of Comparative Human Cognition cite a number of empirical studies that confirm the influence of a complex array of factors on student motivation and performance, including school and home conditions, the presence of strategies to negotiate home and school identity, and positive identification with teachers (2001, p. 981). In addition, researchers have shown a clear correlation among teacher traits, behaviors, and expectations; high student motivation; and academic achievement for students of color (Arroyo, Rhoad, & Drew, 1999; Freel, 1998; Irvine & Armento, 2001; Ladson-Billings, 2000; Zeichner, 1996). Elementary school principal Tate Fischer noted how 4th grade teacher Christie Wyatt positioned herself as an advocate in her students' lives, helping to promote their feelings of self-efficacy. "It's not just black kids," she said. "Christie holds high academic and personal expectations for all children. All kids are asking teachers to 'believe in me,' and she works to ensure that they all believe, 'I can do it.'" Middle school teacher Kevin Friedman explained his approach this way: "With my black students, I have a feeling that my attitude—my strong enthusiasm in math class—is *why* they are successful."

Many researchers attribute low performance to patterns of interpersonal dynamics, linking student self-perception and motivation to teachers' low expectations and negative beliefs. Some believe that institutions such as slavery and separate and unequal school systems fostered persistently low expectations among teachers for their black students (Grant, 1989; Haberman, 1995). Teachers' attitudes can have a devastating effect on students, such as lowering their belief in their achievement capacity and diminishing their self-esteem, motivation, and ultimate academic performance (Freel, 1998; also see Armor, 1997; Wigfield, Galper, & Denton, 1999). PTP educators demonstrate an understanding of these patterns of expectations and achievement outcomes. As middle school teacher Michael Wagner noted, "Many black kids come to see school as a place where they aren't meant to be successful." Middle school principal Darrell Conway was straightforward in his analysis of the impact that race has had on school climate, performance, and achievement for black students:

> The key to having the strategies in our vision such as multiple intelligences, cooperative learning, critical thinking, and technology work with black students

is addressing issues of race. Many people have written about an unspoken belief in our culture that blacks can't learn. We're dead if we can't get past that. We can have a skilled instructional strategist in the classroom, but if that's their belief, we get disproportionality.

Teacher Mick Denby affirmed that his student-centered philosophy, understanding of his students' backgrounds, and acknowledgement that racism exists drove him to inform students about those aspects of their education that he influences: "I let students know that here, it's different. Once students leave, I can't fix what's out there: broken homes, poverty, or no one to help with homework." He stressed that he balanced his "attitude to not be defeated so easily" with his "belief that students have a chance and a choice." He thought that his core motto, "Don't let failure be because you didn't make a choice," had the effect of pumping up his students and encouraging them to believe in themselves.

Focused Energy and High Levels of Confidence

PTP teachers' achievement expectations reflect a serious effort to meet goals and arrive at positive outcomes. According to elementary school teacher Jeffrey Brooks, the key to being effective in the classroom is to do "the best we can to meet all the kids' needs. I think it's just, 'Roll with the best practices.'" After having taught in a program for gifted students, Brooks declared, "What I did for the gifted kids, I do for the regular kids."

Brooks's principal, Owen Callahan, attributed Brooks's success to his "overall philosophy: He believes he can do it." Callahan emphasized, "He has high expectations for kids and high confidence in himself and his capacity to make a difference. He is doing the work he wants to do and is guided by this intent to do what is right for kids. If a kid comes in three years behind, he says, 'Keep the child with me and he'll get caught up.' Brooks knows his craft. He believes he can do it."

Callahan noted that Brooks's feelings, like those of the other teachers at his school, are "not a syrupy sweet thing. There's a big distinction between those syrupy feelings and caring that motivates changes in teaching and learning practices." He saw providing equitable access to opportunities to learn as a school focus. He concluded, "At our school, caring for kids means giving them the skills to do well."

Sharing Confidence and High Expectations with Parents and Students

PTP teachers were purposeful in articulating their high expectations and confidence in students to the people who mattered most: the students and their parents. Middle school principal Kin Hanh Nguyen found that teacher Jessica Wakefield's belief in her capacity to make a difference in her students' educational careers was clear and transparent to her students. "They know that she wants them to get it," said Nguyen. "She sees their failure as her failure as a teacher. The kids know that she believes in them" and is working to promote their self-efficacy: "They never feel she is giving up on them."

Elementary school teacher Christie Wyatt believed that enlisting parents and students in developing children's sense of efficacy takes courage and daring. "I care about my students' success," she said. "I dare to bring them up to where they should be, and it's fun to watch their gains." When she realized that students and parents were anxious about the results of the 3rd grade ITBS scores, she pointed out to them that she used results of early-year classroom-based assessments to attend to student needs on a daily basis. Wyatt reported that she "dared to tell parents the truth about their kids," telling them and the students "to their faces what students are good at and not so good at" based on their performance in the first six weeks of the school year. In the face of anxiety, she said, "I talk about gifts." The students, she said, "are here to work, and I dare to bring them up to where they should be. I had one student who had had a bad 3rd grade experience in the previous year. I found out that she was poor in math. I got her a tutor, and assigned her home activities to supplement our school activities." Wyatt's commitment and daring helped all her 4th graders except one meet success standards on the state reading and mathematics assessment. "I tell them to just stick with me. I'm confident they will do well."

Hard Work, Commitment, and Enjoyment

PTP educators experienced their jobs as requiring hard work, long hours, and high energy—all of which they actually *enjoyed*.

Middle school teacher Susan Lansing said, "I find that I am spending 60 to 70 hours a week at this because I enjoy it. I like doing what I do. It's a burden, but if kids enjoy it, I'm reacting to what they react positively to."

Middle school principal Alex La Chuisa saw the diligence and effort of teachers like Angela Chaffee rub off on her students; motivated by her efforts and beliefs, they reciprocated with efforts of their own. Diana Granger thought that students achieved because of her personal belief that they could "achieve beyond whatever the standards are." Middle school principal Alicia Baldwin noted that one of the strengths that teachers Gillian Novak and Berkeley McGuire shared was a habit of reflection that helped them understand students' backgrounds, plan activities to meet diverse learners' needs, and establish positive relationships with students. Once the teachers get to know the students, said Baldwin, "whatever they ask kids to do, the kids want to do for them."

Aware of the need to create a social context that is conducive to learning, 3rd grade teacher Ryan Toth noted that his enjoyment of his students and his way of balancing classroom routines with excitement contributed to positive personal relationships and helped motivate students to achieve. "I have fun with them," he said. "We do a lot of fun things: go for walks, have success celebrations. It's a bit like life. I work them hard, but they know that in the long run, it's worth it. They learn, and they see results. And for us this year, I'm happy that the results have been that our 3rd grade classes did very well" on district assessments.

The Effects of Perceptions of Self-Efficacy and Self-Reflection on Individual and Schoolwide Innovation

PTP teachers' belief in their capacity to make a difference was grounded in self-reflection. Lisa Forsythe believed that her "being personally reflective" fostered persistence and openness to trying new strategies in response to student needs. She recalled asking herself a series of questions: "What have I heard from peers that might work with my students? Which strategies from recent professional development might be useful? What is my role in this? How did this work with other classes? What do I know about the individuals in this class that suggests that a particular strategy will work? How is this group of students different? Why is this not working? What can I do to change? What have we heard from our principal that is going to help me be dynamic, be flexible?"

Often, teachers don't choose strategies based on individual reflections, but rather on schoolwide initiatives that are chosen or developed by school leadership teams. The leadership at a K–8 alternative school in the PTP study engaged in collaborative conversations to craft a schoolwide approach to selecting "grade-level initiatives aimed at closing the gap." Principal Naira Peet said, "At our grade-level meetings, we articulated and aligned K–8 math curriculum and set literacy goals at the early grades and study skills training and higher-order thinking skills goals at the intermediate level. Our intermediate students have service learning involvement, which helps build an understanding of who they are among the community."

Principal Darrell Conway and teacher Diana Granger attributed achievement gains among black students at their elementary school to the implementation of "a clear, schoolwide vision for success for all students" called "The Big Four," which focused on the use of cooperative learning, multiple intelligences, critical thinking skills and problem-solving abilities, and technology in the school. First, the staff conducted research, read professional development books, and attended discussion retreats related to cooperative learning and multiple intelligences. Granger's observations confirmed what she had seen in her family—that educators "tended to teach in two or three intelligences": the verbal-linguistic, the mathematical-logical, and the intrapersonal. After investigating Howard Gardner's work on multiple intelligences, Granger said that school staff also agreed to include teaching students critical thinking skills and problem-solving abilities. Finally, the staff added technology as a teaching tool because of its pervasiveness in students' lives and its ability to provide students with equitable access to information and resources.

Granger detailed how staff came to embrace the school's vision through self-reflection, professional learning, and collaboration. She noted that as a 30-something white educator entering teaching as a second career after having started a family, she saw great disparities between what students needed to learn and generally accepted educational practices. She observed that her daughter and her "nieces and nephews who were black were likely being left behind in a lot of things." Because of this "questioning of the way education was delivered to the majority of the people," Granger readily embraced the vision that Conway led school staff to develop during restructuring.

According to Granger, once the teachers had become skilled at using The Big Four in their classrooms, they became aware that "for children to become self-directed and empowered in their own education, *the strategies needed to be the curriculum.*" They also found that The Big Four helped students to meet community needs, such as environmental stewardship, with confidence.

Professional Development that Enhances Self-Efficacy and Professional Practices

PTP teachers' self-reflections and their collaboration on self-efficacy development both centered on innovations and sustained practices that would bring about changes in student achievement. Over half of my interviews with PTP educators contained references to the influence of professional learning on their practice. More importantly, to quote principals Alex La Chuisa and Alicia Baldwin, the teachers "actually used what they learned in professional development." As elementary school teacher Michael Wagner noted, "There is, generally, a willingness to dive in and go to trainings." With few exceptions, this assessment is true for all PTP educators.

Elementary school principal Shannon Weller saw teacher Donna Schneider's participation in professional learning as a manifestation of her "consummate professionalism." Diana Granger referred to focused professional development as the "scaffolding teachers need to improve their practice." She attributed sustained student achievement gains at her school to changes her staff made over seven years of professional development to implement The Big Four.

For middle school teacher Chris Spelman, the desire to take advantage of professional learning stemmed from his belief in his capacity to make a difference for his students. He noted that he had altered strategies that he deemed successful during his first couple of years of teaching after attending more training. "I'm as much of a learner as the students," he said. "I try to model for the students where I'm learning." Likewise, middle school principal Kim Hanh Nguyen noted that even though teacher Jessica Wakefield held a master's degree in educational technology, she was "always modeling being a learner, learning and reading about practical applications to include in lessons."

Role and Mastery Expectations

Setting and maintaining clear and high expectations for mastery of content is one of the most commonly cited features of effective and culturally responsive strategies (Arroyo, Rhoad, & Drew, 1999; Delpit, 2000; Freel, 1998; Irvine & Armento, 2001; Ladson-Billings, 2000; Rowan, Chiang, & Miller, 1997; Zeichner, 1996). Researchers have confirmed that high teacher expectations promote motivation and a commitment to achieve and learn content among students (Arroyo, Rhoad, & Drew, 1999; Hollins, 1982). When asked to what they would attribute the success of their black students, PTP educators were unanimous: high expectations for themselves and kids. Third grade teacher Ryan Toth noted that his students were clearly aware of his beliefs and high expectations: "I tend to be a rather emotional person; they know my expectations and they relate to that."

Holding Students to District and State Standards

The PTP educators asserted that they held all students to the same high standards, both academic and personal, regardless of their backgrounds. "Seventy-five percent of our population is lower-income students," said Jessica Wakefield. "Kids say they are responsible for babysitting after school or have no homes. I tell them, 'I look at all students as individuals.' I'm going to help them achieve. I tell them that even if they have *no* homes, I hold the same high expectations for everyone—'I'm going to help you achieve. I accept no excuses for not being able to participate.'" Following up on that promise, Wakefield sought support such as tutoring to ensure that her students had equal access to learning opportunities.

Principal Darrell Conway explained how teachers at his elementary school came to hold a similar position. "In the past, some of us felt sorry for black students because of the circumstances of their lives," he said. "But we learned that we needed to demand the work from all our kids. We now have the mentality to push all kids hard—to demand that they get in there and get the work done." Again Conway emphasized the need "to admit that race is an issue" when educators hold disparate expectations.

One principal I interviewed, Riley Portman, recalled that some of the classrooms in his school were very safe, orderly, and organized, with "no down time for messing around," but that "work was not up to the level I wanted for them or thought they could do." In Portman's view, failing to hold all students to established standards constituted a disservice to students of color. He disparaged educators' lowering expectations and giving students work on which they could be successful in order "to make them feel good," concluding that such practices amounted to "intentional, subtle, institutionalized racism."

Equitable Access to Resources and Opportunities to Learn

PTP educators met students' needs by providing them with equitable access to resources and opportunities to learn regardless of academic gaps or needs, ensuring that all students had access not only to regular education classrooms, but also to placement in gifted-student programs and to academic intervention programs.

Many schoolwide programs proceeded from schoolwide philosophies. Darrell Conway noted how his school's philosophy drove a focus on equity: "Diana Granger often led staff discussions on the disproportionate amounts of time that students 'at risk of failure,' many of whom live in poverty, got in instruction," he said. Conway's staff concluded "that with our current school funding scheme, those children 'at risk of failure' bring in more money, so they should be getting more instruction time."

Conway recalled that these had "been tough conversations," with many parents of many white students insisting on equal time for their kids. In response, according to Conway, "Our teachers asserted their philosophy, 'No, your child will get *quality* time.'" Conway said that his school's approach addressed disproportionality by holding "high expectations for all kids, and providing equitable, not equal, opportunities for all children."

According to Diana Granger, staff at her school doubled the reading and writing instruction time for students who needed it. In addition, the school provided differentiated instruction featuring fluid movement between projects, guided instructional groups, and skill-building centers to accommodate children's needs. In the centers, "Children apply and really get their hands on those kinds of skills that we're trying to get across," Granger said. "We'll have smaller guided groups to teach about writing skills, such as the use of quotation marks in dialogue, or a guided group to give double time to lower readers, or to have conference time with writers who might be really good at their paragraph transitions but need some instruction on specific literary devices and using figurative language."

Middle school teacher Carla Storey's science classes exemplified her school's philosophy of providing access to regular education classes for students in special education, behavior-disabled inclusion, and English as Second Language programs. Fully 75 percent of her students were in special education, and though it was challenging, she managed to teach them an inquiry-based science curriculum in a laboratory setting.

Elementary school principal Patrice Tam reported that, at her school, addressing equitable access to programs meant diversifying the populations admitted to the school's "Spectrum" program for highly capable students through blending. Tam increased the number of students admitted to the program by employing school-level reading assessments as criteria for selection in addition to district-level assessments. According to Chan, the resulting Spectrum program included 11 out of 28 students who the district had claimed were ineligible.

At his middle school, principal Alex La Chuisa observed that his teachers provided students with equitable access to opportunities for meeting their needs because they saw all students "as capable and motivated regardless of their backgrounds or learning styles." Special education students and English language learners at the school were regularly enrolled in regular education classes with teachers like Angela Chaffee, a highly qualified teacher who also taught honors classes. The school also provided after-school interventions, such as a math study group led by Chaffee, for students who demonstrated the greatest needs.

Teacher Ryan Toth recounted that the staff at his elementary school used the Read Naturally computer program for assisted learning to afford students equitable access to reading instruction. Using the program's trained adult tutors and small groups essentially reduced the teacher-student ratio in classes from 1-to-28 to 1-to-7. Toth believed that the resulting increase in one-on-one time with tutors and teachers was particularly helpful to students, and that students were afforded a greater sense of their individual roles in mastering learning outcomes as they progressed individually through the program's computer-assisted lessons. In addition to using the Read Naturally program, Toth would move his class from his small, movable classroom to the lunchroom for reading aloud—a move that he found helped engage and motivate his students.

Middle school vice principal Claire Beauvais saw teacher Moira Reynolds accommodating for differences in students' abilities as she progressed through group lessons. Reynolds noted that many of her "black students who had closed achievement gaps were hooked into the University of Washington's Early Scholars Opportunity Program [ESOP]." (The ESOP program pairs college-bound, primarily minority students with college-age mentors for tutoring or simply to discuss what college is like, what's needed to get there, and why it's important. In addition to promoting student self-efficacy and academic growth, ESOP makes the dream of a college future an incentive for students.)

One of the first steps Alicia Baldwin saw teacher Berkeley McGuire taking to ensure equitable access to resources and opportunities was to become deeply aware of her students' backgrounds. Once she had done so, Baldwin said that McGuire invested considerable time in "looking at what they individually needed regardless of race or ethnic background, then presenting background knowledge to bring kids up to the same experience as their counterparts—leveling the playing field." McGuire's strategy was especially helpful for some of her "poorest kids—black, Cambodian, and Laotian kids in particular."

Baldwin also noted teacher Marian Katz's implementation of a widely used intervention: skills-based study groups within the context of a block-scheduled classroom. Although Baldwin found this approach unusual at middle school level, she also saw that it was "absolutely beneficial" for Katz's black students because it offered them instruction in the exact skills that they needed to address demonstrated deficits.

Fourth grade teacher Mark Donnelly's efforts to provide equitable responses to his students' needs took him all the way to their homes. "It's easy to blame a student's home life," he said. "However, in my experience with different students, parents care. I went to one student's home in the morning to talk to his parents and found that it was hard for him to study at home. Because I try to ignore a failure mentality and give all my students a chance, we worked out a plan for him to arrive early to study with a student tutor at school."

Middle school teacher Charles Ackerman and 6th grade teacher Danielle Kaplan also found one-on-one time to be a must for students who needed help with basic skills in mathematics, although Kaplan lamented that, too often, in the context of her regular classroom, "there was just enough time to tell kids what they didn't do." To compensate, Kaplan felt compelled to "write back to [the students] in their math journals."

To help build meaningful collaboration with parents, middle school teacher Kevin Friedman personalized planning agendas that he sent home with specific comments and requests for input and narrowly defined homework assignments that increased the likelihood of student success (e.g., "Identify three ways to select a sample for data collection in statistics.").

Fostering Student Self-Efficacy and Responsibility

PTP educators focused on strengthening students' self-efficacy through personal communication and daily interaction, ensuring that students understood their personal roles in content mastery, task completion, and achievement of realistic academic standards.

Relationships: Essential to Motivation and Achievement

PTP educators explained how the social and cultural aspects of the teacher-student relationship were essential to student motivation and achievement. As middle school teacher Lisa Forsythe reflected, the personal relationship between teacher and student reinforces motivation and student effort—when students know that teachers care about them completing learning tasks, they are more likely to do so.

Fourth grade teacher Christie Wyatt also established a close relationship with her students, reminding them of their individual roles in content mastery by writing personalized notes and leaving them on their desks. The notes "pointed out their strengths and weak points" and reminded them that although the work would be challenging, she had confidence in their ability to succeed. That the students often kept the notes showed Wyatt how meaningful they were.

Changing Typical and Expected Social and Academic Interactions

Middle school teacher David Maslin used his understanding of how race changes "the dynamic that typically occurs in school for students who are from groups that have typically been oppressed" to help his students achieve. For example, he rejected the notion that "the teacher [will be] in command and the student is subordinate." Instead, he balanced teacher-centered presentations to the whole class with reciprocal teaching episodes in which his 7th and 8th graders took on the role of teachers. Maslin noted that although the students "can see that I have more life experiences because I'm older," he built trust by "showing that I can learn from them, for example, when we write poetry or read books [focused on multicultural themes]."

According to middle school teacher Angela Chaffee, "You have to go in the classroom and say, 'These kids are going to do well. I don't care what's going on in their lives. They have to.' If they have all this other stuff going against them—potentially at home—the teacher still has to say to them, 'You have to become more powerful as a learner and more responsible for your education. If you can do that, your life has no limits.'" She said that she helped her students to see her as someone charged with providing doors of opportunity for them by "giving them as many skills and concepts as possible." Similarly, 6th grade teacher Danielle Kaplan coached her students to push themselves beyond self-imposed limits by encouraging them to understand that there's always more to achieve, and that perseverance is *always* necessary.

Curriculum and Development of Student Self-Efficacy

PTP educators strongly believed that the curriculum and structures they employed helped strengthen students' beliefs in self-efficacy and abilities to achieve. Middle school teacher Mick Denby scaffolded students' self-efficacy development by having them repeat the following pledge every morning:

> One: Work hard, for hard work makes excellent results.
> Two: Study hard, for good study habits build a strong mind.
> Three: Respect everyone, for in return you will receive respect.
> And four: Do your best in everything you do, for to do otherwise is to do nothing.

Denby had learned the pledge from a special education teacher two years prior. At the beginning of the year, Denby had his students write down and reflect both orally and in writing on the meaning of the pledge. To Denby, the pledge had the effect of "making students feel pumped up [and] believe in themselves."

Elementary school principal Shannon Weller felt that the curriculum and structures at her school's Montessori program helped all her students learn at an early age how to be successful and self-directed in school. For many students, success in school begins with understanding patterns of interaction that may vary significantly from what they experience in their neighborhoods or homes. Weller recalled that Montessori's clear boundaries, support for those boundaries, and focus on self-direction starting at age three both demonstrated and encouraged appropriate engagement among students. "What we've done is create classrooms where there is little opportunity for failure for any of our kids and a win-win situation for kids and for teachers," she said.

Diana Granger believed that becoming reflective was a key element of student self-efficacy development. She and her team members persistently used such sentence frames as, "Why do you think . . . ?" to provoke reflection. She saw that such questioning drove students to consider possibilities and freed educators from the limits they placed on what "kids can do and how much they can learn." She found self-reflective questions to be especially helpful with her students of color. Because such students are "not shut down at the get-go, because they are able to access whatever they're strong in, [self-reflection] reduces the likelihood that a student will say, 'I guess I'm not as smart as that person over there.'"

Ryan Toth credited the aforementioned Read Naturally program with instilling a sense of independence in students and an understanding of their individual roles in mastering the reading curriculum. The thrice-weekly program, which features a small-group tutoring component conducted with parents and teachers, computer-based instruction, teacher reading, repeated student reading, and progress monitoring, requires students to take part in guided reading instruction to learn vocabulary, increase fluency, and improve comprehension skills. Toth reported that parents, students, and teachers loved the program: In addition to providing an opportunity for students to improve reading skills, it demonstrated a meaningful collaboration with highly trained parents who tutored students in the teacher-directed model, listened to them read aloud, assisted them as they read and wrote responses to onscreen computer prompts, and managed the reports of their progress. Toth commended the program's parent coordinator as a highly efficient manager who provided bimonthly spreadsheets showing the number of stories read and analyses of each student's performance. Toth also lauded students' abilities to become "totally independent by the third week of the program. The kids know it; they run it themselves." He recalled that "three times a year, we'd work out a point system for all [the students'] completed work. It has to do with focusing work, not grades. Everybody sees the points earned and wants to move on. This energizes the other kids."

Shared Responsibility for Teaching and Learning

Third grade teacher Mark Goldberg noted that promoting self-efficacy in elementary school helps students to "become autonomous and take responsibility for their own learning." Goldberg felt that student self-talk such as "'Yes, I did this; not the teacher, not my learning partner'" fostered "a sense of empowerment and responded to students' love of being successful." In other words, assuming responsibility for positive and negative outcomes helped students to build an internal locus of control and intrinsic motivation. According to Goldberg, developing a sense of responsibility has a twofold effect: Students are "able to attribute success to their individual efforts and take compliments much better, saying 'Thank you' rather than 'Oh, I didn't do it,'" and they "learn to make more choices that move them forward without the guidance of the teacher. That goes a long way to building their esteem and their motivation to work on their own."

Allowing students to make developmentally appropriate choices is a strategy that middle school teacher Chris Spelman found particularly effective with his black students. He found that given choices, students "seemed to respond more positively." Third grade teacher Kimberly Lazarides also found that students' interest and motivation were higher, and they ultimately were exposed to a greater variety of modes and genres of writing when she gave students a choice.

Middle school teacher David Lee shared the responsibility for his students' progress with students and their parents or caregivers. He posted daily score charts and weekly progress reports on his wall, using student ID numbers to preserve student anonymity, and conducted biweekly conversations with students to strengthen caring relationships centered on student achievement. Lee continually "stressed each individual student's responsibility to achieve what he or she is capable of attaining related to district standards and their own goals." According to Lee, this focus helped his students to be self-motivated.

A Virtual Walk through David Maslin's 8th Grade Algebra Lesson

As two teams of teachers enter David Maslin's racially diverse classroom, they notice that almost all the students are wearing the school uniform: an oversized white polo shirt and black slacks or blue jeans. There are a total of 16 students, four of whom are female. A district communication standards poster is mounted on the classroom door. At the front of the room is Maslin himself: Twenty-something, a head shorter than most of his students, and smiling cheerfully. He takes a set of 3-by-5-inch index cards from a shirt pocket and tells the students that they will be working on problems in their math journals or on a separate piece of paper in their binders. Mr. Marques, the tall, black teacher's aide, enters the room and quietly walks to the back of the classroom. As he does so, he quietly nods to or places a hand on the shoulder of three students whom he passes.

Students seem interested in the lesson, scurrying to sit at tables in groups of two or three. At a center aisle table, Tuleah, a student of Asian American and Pacific Islander descent, stops talking with Akeela and sits down next to her, while Keith, who is black, tosses the binder he had been using during the class's previous lesson into a box on a side table reserved for literature journals. At the same time, Akil, an immigrant from North Africa who has recently joined mainstream classes, scoots his chair backwards to join Truong and Ennis at their table in the row near the windows. Maslin has put structures in place to support small-group work where students develop their expertise, and students' movements show that they know their roles and responsibilities for completing tasks.

Maslin's classroom is safe and orderly and provides students with access to current materials and technology. A large fern sits beside Maslin's desk. Along the wall to the right of the desk, there is a long table holding the teacher's computer along with a bank of student computers and printers, as well as clipboards holding directions for operating the machines and storing files. A Word Wall featuring 15 important mathematics terms is situated above and to the left of the blackboard on which Maslin is beginning to write an algebraic expression. The Word Wall includes such terms as "grid," "x-axis," "y-axis," "abscissa," "negative," and "sum" written on oblong pieces of colored construction paper. An agenda written in colored chalk on the blackboard publicizes the upcoming AlgebraThon and Summer Math Lab and announces that Monday is Sports Day, Tuesday is Twins Day, Wednesday is Backwards Day, Thursday is Crazy Hair Day, and Friday is Pajama Day— events of great interest to students that add excitement to the routine of school. A bulletin board next to the blackboard displays geometric designs from South America and materials that outline the contributions that different cultures have made to the field of mathematics. The bulletin board also displays samples of student work, which also cover three walls of the classroom, as do posters showing the district mathematics, reading, and writing standards and graphic organizers.

An overhead projector cart in the center of the room faces the blackboard and a TV monitor is affixed to the wall next to the clock to the left of the door, but Maslin will use only his voice and chalk for today's lesson. He erases vocabulary words and ideas about the poems the class discussed prior to the algebra lesson from the chalkboard. "I've got a few problems for us to try," he says. "We're going to do them one at a time, together . . . and work through some of this new stuff . . . to be sure we're all on the same page." He breaks up each phrase with a short pause. Rather than having students "cover" a large number of problems, Maslin engages them in achieving a deep understanding of a few selected problems. He has structured the content and activities in this lesson to actively engage students and solidify their learning of mastered material.

Casually scratching his head, Maslin advances toward Malik's table and glances at Malik's journal. Listening quietly, Malik follows Maslin with his eyes as he returns to the board, faces the class, and says, "I want you to try to use the written method as much as you can with these."

Tuleah darts to her seat, bending her six-foot frame as she crosses in front of Maslin, raising her hand apologetically. Maslin has developed positive relationships with his students, which can be seen in the way they treat each other: with civility, gentleness, and support.

To scaffold the transition between his students' prior experience using manipulatives and his new expectations for written solutions, Maslin says, "We want to start phasing out the materials, the blocks, the pieces, whenever possible." He raises his hands to his chest, palms outward as if revealing on them the meaning of his words, and explains: "You won't always have those materials, so if you can start to see doing your work without 'em, do it. If you need 'em, if you get stuck, definitely use 'em. There's nothing wrong with that; they'll help you out. But when you can, sometimes it's faster not to use 'em."

Almost all of Maslin's students listen silently as he talks. He continues: "So think about that, and also—I'll leave it at that. Let's try these one at a time. If you get it, try not to shout out the answer. I'll come around to see how you're doing, and we'll have people show how you did these." He flips through his index cards and says, "While you're doing them, think about how you're doing them in case you have to explain 'em to us." In this way, Maslin ensures that students understand their individual roles in content mastery and task completion.

By this time, Maslin has finished writing the equation on the board:

$$2 * + 3 = -6 + X$$

Placing the index cards back in his shirt pocket, he says, "We'll start with some easy ones, and then go on from there." Through this scaffolding and gradual increase in task difficulty, students, regardless of learning gaps or needs, are provided equitable access to opportunities to learn challenging content. At this point, Tuleah asks, "So is it a game?" It becomes clear that the class is accustomed to learning mathematics by approaching

problems as games. Maslin responds, "No, it's not exactly a game. We're just gonna work some problems together to be sure we're all on the same page." Another student sighs with disappointment.

The next exchange confirms that routines in Maslin's class are balanced with excitement. Several students, led by Tuleah, negotiate with Maslin to "play a game on Friday, like the buzzer game." Maslin notes that the buzzer game is similar to "the X game," in which students solve equations for the variable X. He informs his students that to develop the X game, he'll have to "stay up late to put it together." He allows his students to share control of the lesson planning, ending with, "You're asking a lot of me."

A student named Germaine shows his interest by volunteering to help Maslin: "I can do it for you," he says. Rashan, who is seated behind Germaine and Tuleah, shows his interest in working on the game for Friday, but reconsiders mid-sentence, making an excuse for not being able to help: "You know, I would do it for you, but. . . ." Rashan's voice trails off as Maslin announces, "I can probably prepare the game for Friday." This exchange demonstrates how Maslin maintains his students' interest in the class by planning engaging activities such as the "X game" while simultaneously keeping them focused on the content and purpose of the lesson.

Immediately after reaching a mutual agreement that they will have the X game on Friday, Maslin directs his students' attention to the collaborative solution of the algebra problem. At this school, the expectation is that students will work with their peers in a reciprocal teaching approach, helping each other with most learning tasks. Maslin has formatted his lesson according to his students' preferences for working in groups. While the students work together, Maslin circulates, providing instruction, offering individual assistance, and probing students' responses. He begins near the door, where he announces, "I'm seeing some good stuff. Take your time." He makes frequent informal assessments of students' progress, which guide his feedback and interventions.

We see examples of the students' interest in their learning: Ennis responds, "You were right" to his partner, and Germaine raises his hand to request help from the teacher aide. The small-group work in which the students are engaged allows them to use their collective knowledge as a basis for inquiry and to develop expertise.

As he discusses the problem with the teacher aide, we hear Ennis exclaim: "Is it minus six? Oh, crap!" Truong reveals his confusion: "I thought it was minus six instead of negative six." Maslin stops to talk to Craig about the operations he is using. Maslin asks each of his students to provide substantive oral and written responses that will advance deeper understanding. When Craig says, "There was a two out front," Maslin makes a quick assessment and replies, "Oh, you had two negatives, I see. That's okay, two stars. That's all right."

As Maslin leaves Craig, Keith calls him over. "I got to talk to you, dawg. I want to talk about my work." Familiar and at ease with his students' expressions. Maslin leans over Keith's desk and looks at his work. We hear Keith say, "Negative six plus six," to which

Maslin nods. Keith goes on, "I have to get this X out of there." Pointing at Keith's paper, Maslin agrees. "You have to get this X out of here. Get this two on this side and this X on this side." Moving on to Akeela, Maslin says, "You're just adding three to this side. You've got to add three on that side, too." Demonstrating the civility and support that are typical in this class, Brianna raises her hand, and with an "Excuse me," asks the aide over for assistance.

Maslin returns to the left side of the room and takes a seat on the edge of Malik's desk. Smiling, he quietly prompts Malik: "That's a good idea; what are you gonna do with it?" When Malik responds, Maslin raises his hands palms up, as if to say, "Eureka! There you are," then points at Malik as if to say, "There you go! You've got it!" In exchanges like this one, Maslin demonstrates his knowledge of the communication styles of the cultural groups in his classroom. During Maslin's exchange with Malik, another student can be heard proclaiming to the whole class: "X equals three!"

Maslin moves on to Ennis, Akil, and Truong's table, which has been joined by Rashan. Again revealing his positive relationship with his students, Maslin leans in close, placing both hands on the table. After quickly reviewing the students' work, Maslin provides the feedback they need to proceed with the solution. "Check your check," he says to Ennis.

Elsewhere in the classroom, Tuleah is heard to say, "I'm done." Germaine retorts, "What! You're done before me?!" "I'm done 'cuz I'm smart," says Tuleah. Germaine pushes Tuleah's head aside with his hand. Tuleah responds by enforcing the classroom's expectation of mutual civility, gentleness, and support, pushing Germaine's hand away and saying, "Stop!" "I ain't dumb, you know," she asserts with a smile. "I'm very smart!" Her interest in the algebra problem prompts her to engage the students at a nearby table: "David, Brianna, what did you get? Did you get X equals three?"

Back at Ennis and Truong's table, Maslin discovers that the partners have different solutions, so he provides them with some feedback. He says to Ennis, "That looks good; oh, your star is negative." Then he turns to Truong and says, "Okay, yours is—check your signs. Look back through it. Look at what signs you used; your positive and negative might have gotten switched somewhere." Turning back to Ennis, he says, "Look at your check; you say X is three, then negative six plus three. . . ." Continuing to probe for extended and substantive oral responses and asking leading questions rather than giving students the answer, Maslin says, "Think again, what's negative six plus three?" His aim here is to scaffold and gradually transfer learning responsibilities to students, and to teach them to self-monitor. Truong offers, "Negative six plus three; it's three." Rashan asks, "How does that help us?"

As Maslin starts walking away from the table, Truong asks again, "Negative six plus three, right?" "Yeah," replies Maslin. Akil, his voice full of certainty, says, "Three," while Ennis probes further, "So you make that negative?" Maslin replies, "I don't know. You tell me." Truong's comeback is confident: "Yes!"

Brianna and Antoinette giggle and cover their faces with their hands as Maslin approaches their table in the back of the room. While he looks at their work, Tuleah,

Germaine, and Malik can be heard heatedly debating Malik's chances of making the varsity football team. "You are *not* going to make varsity football," says Tuleah. "I'm gonna start junior varsity!" responds Malik. Germaine's retort is heavy with sarcasm: "Start. Oh, *start!* Nobody said nothing about *start.*"

Back at Brianna and Antoinette's table, Maslin is oblivious to the football debate. He and Antoinette agree that she will explain the solution to the class. Returning to the blackboard, he directs Antoinette to begin: "Okay, Antoinette, the first step." Antoinette begins, "Um, six and the —," but is distracted by the football discussion, which has gotten louder. Maslin walks over to Tuleah, Germaine, and Malik and makes a "keep it down" gesture with his hand. His explicit coaching on appropriate behavior is delivered using appropriate adult/teacher language that allows students to retain the respect of their peers. Firmly and quietly he says, "I'm going to ask you both to help." When the students stop talking within a few seconds, he responds, "Okay, that's better. All right. Thank you." Then, he returns his attention to Antoinette: "Antoinette, go ahead."

Antoinette's solution demonstrates her understanding of operations as well as her confidence, humor, and innovativeness. The extended, substantive explanation she provides allows her to share an important role in the class's learning. She ends by saying, "Since there's an X over on the right side, I added one on the left side and got 2 * + X + 3." Maslin asks, "Added an X to both sides?" With a note of confidence in her voice, Antoinette replies, "No." She gives Maslin directions until he responds, "Yeah. So you added a star *and* an X" and writes the following on the board:

3 * + 3 = -6
X + *

"Yes, I *know* that!" says Antoinette, to which Maslin nods, demonstrating his understanding of modal communication and linguistics styles. Smiling now, Maslin and Antoinette use the additive and multiplicative inverse operations to solve the equation. Maslin makes changes on the board as Antoinette responds, "Yeah, I got 3 * + X + 3 = -6 + X." She then asks Maslin, "Can you just subtract X on both sides?" Answering "I'd be happy to," Maslin crosses out the X on both sides of the equation:

3 * + X + 3 = -6 + X.

Antoinette continues, "And then you have 3 * + 3 = -6." Maslin agrees: "That leaves us with 3 * + 3." Antoinette finishes his sentence as Maslin subtracts three from each side of the equation. She warns Maslin that he is "one step ahead" of her, and he responds, "No, I'm right with you." Antoinette continues, "I then placed -3 on the left side and did the same thing on the right side." Maslin writes this operation on the board:

3 * + 3 = -6
-3   -3

Antoinette goes on: "And we're left with 3 * = -9." Divide by 3 and you get * = -3, so X = 3."

This episode of reciprocal teaching, in which Antoinette assumes the role of teacher,

is designed to help students construct meaning in learning situations. As Antoinette gives Maslin the final directions for solving the equation, he writes down the solution and the two of them read it out loud together: "* = -3, and X = 3." The students' reactions signal their clear interest in the lesson. Tuleah shouts, "Whoa! I got that! We got it right." Rashan and others ask, "What's the check? What's the check?" and Ennis responds, "-3 = -3."

Maslin writes "Check" above the solution and asks Antoinette to "take us through the check." Sounding tired, Antoinette explains: "So it says, two star times three is negative six, So that's negative six. Plus three equals negative three. And then it says negative six plus X." As she talks, Maslin writes -6 and -3 on the board and points with an exaggerated motion to the right side of the equation. Simultaneously with Antoinette, he says, "And it says negative six plus X." Antoinette finishes Maslin's statement: "And X equals three, so I got positive three because I acted like the plus sign wasn't there and I subtracted." The explication is over when Maslin asks rhetorically, "Positive or negative?" and writes "-3 = -3" in a circle under the word "Check" on the board.

Tuleah again announces, "I got it! That. I got that right!" Maslin commends her and the other students' efforts: "Yes, I saw some good work as you were solving this first one." He has used his frequent and continuous assessments of the students' work today to determine skills and knowledge acquisition and to provide feedback and interventions. Continuing to promote Antoinette in the expert role, he asks the class: "Any questions? Any questions for Antoinette?"

"How did she get so smart?" asks Tuleah— a curious question, since Tuleah herself had found the correct solution to the problem. Maslin responds by restating the question: "How *did* she become so smart?"

"Can we do another one?" asks Ennis. Because of the chatter in the classroom, Maslin doesn't hear him and replies, "Huh?" Ennis repeats the question. This time Maslin acknowledges his contribution to planning the class's activities and replies, "Next one." Joking, Tuleah snorts, "Again?"

After asking if there are any more questions, Maslin erases the board using comically exaggerated gestures that make the students laugh. Chuckling, he takes his index cards from his pocket and shuffles through them looking for a new problem. "Here's one of my popular problems," he announces, as one of his students lets out a whistle.

Grounded in a belief in his students' abilities, Maslin has structured his lesson to ensure that it is attainable and will strengthen students' growing sense of self-efficacy and positive self-regard.

Walkthrough Wrap-Up

Following the walkthrough, the two teams gather in the hallway outside Maslin's classroom and take a few minutes to make checks next to strategies that they observed on their individual feedback forms and to add to the notes they made. Then, led by the facilitator's prompts, the observers each share the notes that they wrote at the bottom of their forms, in the section titled "What Teachers/Students Say/Do Related to the Focus Area." Here's what the teachers found:

Teacher 1
Focus: Self-Efficacy
Findings: Teacher 1 found that Maslin demonstrated a belief in his students' abilities and structured his lesson to ensure that it strengthened students' growing sense of self-efficacy in solving equations.

Teacher 2
Focus: Teacher-Student Interactions
Findings: Teacher 2 noted that interactions were overwhelmingly positive in Maslin's class. Evidence for this could be seen in Maslin's cheerful smile and jokes, in the way Tuleah politely excused herself when crossing in front of Maslin while he was teaching, in the students' use of respectful language, and in the way the students laughed at Maslin's jokes.

Teacher 3
Focus: Classroom Management and Student Discipline
Findings: Teacher 3 noted that when students disrupted Antoinette's demonstration of the solution to the algebra problem, Maslin explicitly coached proper behavior using appropriate language and asked the offending students to accept mutual responsibility for maintaining the classroom environment. Teacher 3 thought it was clear that the students cared about what went on in class, as indicated by how quickly the disruptive students quieted down, and noted that Maslin demonstrated that he valued his students' cooperation by thanking them when they complied with his request for order.

Teacher 4

Focus: Cultural Competence

Findings: Teacher 4 noted that Maslin demonstrated his familiarity with the communication styles of the cultural groups in his classroom on many occasions, citing as one example his use of encouraging hand gestures when helping Malik, thus supporting Malik's self-efficacy development and further cementing their positive relationship.

Teacher 5

Focus: Cultural Congruence

Findings: Teacher 5 noted that Maslin's familiarity and comfort with his students' use of language allowed him to respond with ease when Keith referred to him as "dawg," and that his cultural competence seemed to help him balance routine class work with activities such as the Friday "X game" and actions such as the exaggerated erasing gestures.

Teacher 6

Focus: Cooperative Learning

Findings: Teacher 6 noticed that Maslin had put structures in place to support small-group work where students develop their expertise, that he clearly expected students to assist each other when solving the algebra problem, and that he appeared to have determined the format for his lesson by taking into account his students' preference for group work. Teacher 6 also noted that Maslin

expected his students to assume individual roles in content mastery and task completion, as evidenced by his saying, "So let's try these one at a time. If you get it, try not to shout out the answer. I'll come around to see how you're doing, and we'll have people show how you did these." The teacher also noted that Maslin demonstrated a collaborative approach to learning by circulating the room to offer students assistance and probe their responses.

Teacher 7

Focus: Procedures for Rehearsal, Processing, and Transfer of New Learning

Findings: Teacher 7 noticed that Maslin called for extended, substantive oral and written student responses that would advance deeper understanding, and that he had structured the lesson content and activities to actively engage students. This teacher found that Maslin sustained students' active learning through questions and explanations, and that he gradually increased the task difficulty to keep students engaged, as evidenced from his comment near the start of the walkthrough: "We'll start with some easy ones, and then go on from there." At the end of class, Ennis showed clear interest in increasing his self-efficacy about what they were learning by asking, "Can we do another one?"

Clearly, Maslin's approach had worked.

2

Student-Teacher Social Interactions

In this chapter, we will examine how the PTP educators implemented the following strategies:

Category: Caring

Strategies: Teachers . . .
- Create inviting environments that reflect personal caring.
- Develop positive, personal relationships with students.
- Encourage a sense of family and community.
- Stress collectiveness and collaboration, rather than individuality, in interactions.
- Listen to and encourage mutual sharing of personal experiences related to curriculum.
- Provide mentoring and emotional support.
- Extend relationships with and caring for students beyond the classroom.

Category: Fairness and Respect

Strategies: Teachers . . .
- Base interactions on human dignity principles, respect for every person, and an attitude of hope and optimism.
- Create situations for all students to succeed.
- Promote student interactions based on principles of democracy, equity, and justice.

Category: Low Favoritism

Strategies: Teachers . . .

- Treat all students equally well.
- Provide each student with equitable access to learning resources and opportunities to learn.

Category: Low Friction

Strategies: Teachers . . .

- Ensure that students and teachers treat each other with civility, gentleness, and support.
- Handle disagreements with discussion and respect for alternative positions.

Caring

In *The Courage to Teach,* Parker Palmer notes that "good teachers [and leaders] possess a capacity for connectedness"—they weave connections between themselves and their students on "the loom of the heart" (1997, p. 11). PTP educators expressed this type of connection by aligning with their students to help them meet high expectations and abiding by an ethic of caring that held fulfilling relationships as a primary goal. Indeed, PTP educators attributed their success with black students to their capacity for establishing a context for learning grounded in positive teacher-student relationships. "It's about relationships," said middle school principal Alex La Chuisa. "I tell all my teachers that one of the most important things is to connect and bond with kids."

Middle school teacher Lisa Forsythe further noted that the teacher-student "social relationship reinforces motivation and effort"—a view that is firmly supported by the research (see, for example, Arroyo, Rhoad, & Drew, 1999; Haycock, 1998; and Noguera & Akom, 2000). She said that she worked to create an atmosphere of family and community that was "friendly for everyone—teacher and kids" because of the positive influence it had on students' efforts. "I think the kids must see that the classroom is not just a room they just come in and out of," she said. She recalled that one of the most powerful techniques that she and her peers used was that of projecting "friendly and upbeat attitudes with the kids . . . We never had a problem with going in there and telling the kids when they'd done really well."

Elementary school principal Patrick Molvig spoke for the majority of PTP educators when he said that he found "the ability to connect with kids" to be one of the most effective strategies for teaching black students. He pointed to 3rd grade teacher Ryan Toth, a "warm and welcoming person" who showed respect for all his students, as an example, noting that his interactions with students were always grounded in the principle of human dignity. According to elementary school principal Tate Fischer, PTP teachers connected with students on a deep level that helped them to move students forward socially and academically: "It's that soul work, the heart piece, the spiritual side of our relationships, which makes kids feel safer and makes them feel that their world is consistent. Some of it is spoken, some unspoken; in either case, kids feel it. It is the people-to-people piece."

Researchers have found that "about 9 out of 10 teachers in integrated schools" are white females from mostly suburban communities where they have had little contact with either poor or black students (Irvine & Armento, 2001, p. 3). As a result, they have low expectations for students from those demographic backgrounds, and often allocate disciplinary action disproportionately. When elementary school principal Mai Pham reflected on 3rd grade teacher Andrew Bean's success with black students, she recalled his leadership in helping to develop schoolwide strategies to address disproportionate disciplinary referrals: "Our principal strategy was to watch closely and document whether all referrals were of black kids or of other kids." Pham talked with teachers who had made referrals twice or more per week, noted reasons for referrals, and had the students "write about why they got so mad, got into trouble, and what would help them."

Conversations about How Caring Manifests Itself

Middle school principal Kim Hanh Nguyen attributed teacher Jessica Wakefield's influence on the achievement of her black students to "her demeanor," her demonstrating that she is caring, and her creating an inviting climate that was "open to kids." Her positive personal relationships with students were reciprocated in their spontaneous demonstrations of caring for her. Nguyen believed that the sense of family and community in Wakefield's class and her influence on students was demonstrated by an event that occurred while she was absent on leave during a difficult pregnancy: "Just out of the blue, kids were praying for her. They weren't mad she was gone, but they missed her. They really cared for her. When one student was

not cooperating with the substitute teacher, one of the kids told another, 'You don't want to talk to Ms. Wakefield while she's on her couch.'" Nguyen marveled at the fact that students didn't want the substitute to deliver a negative report about them to Ms. Wakefield and distress her further while she was on leave. Their sense of caring for Wakefield "was still affecting the way kids behaved although she was out!"

When middle school principal Alicia Baldwin reflected on teacher Carla Storey, she first noted that her ethnicity was an asset. "I think it's great to have a phenomenal black teacher like Carla," she said. For the most part, though, she attributed Storey's success with students to her caring approach: "She's delightful. She's about relationships." Baldwin also found that Storey tempered her care with firmness when managing student behavior: "The kids like her and they know not to cross her." Storey herself recalled that she held a lot of one-on-one conferences with her students. She pointed out that she extended caring beyond the classroom by spending time with students during lunch. In addition, she made it a point to identify students' individual strengths so that she could "commend them on their genius" during pep talks.

"As a black person, I have an advantage," said Storey. "I shared problems blacks have if they're not getting their behavior together." She believed that by demonstrating caring and recognizing students' efforts she helped students to develop a belief in their self-efficacy and increased the likelihood that they achieve goals. "If you care, they will perform for you," she said. "My relationship with students is something they are looking for."

Middle school teacher Moira Reynolds also believed that the relationship she established with students was something for which they "were hungry." She started every school year in much the same way as Storey: "I try to make a point to talk individually with every student, particularly at the beginning of the year, just to check in with them." In addition to approaching her after school for help with homework, many of Reynolds's students sought out her caring company "just to hang out." She recalled that "a lot of kids would just come and stay for five minutes after class to chit-chat for a while."

Bridget Lawley and Cyndi Alexander—principal and assistant principal, respectively, at Chief Seattle Dwamish Middle School—believed that teacher David Lee's ethnic background helped students relate to him. "Because he's a person of color, he's able to adopt his students' perspectives and demonstrate that he understands the impact of race," said Lawley. Alexander noted that "he's very attuned, and knows that kids see themselves in him, and he sees himself in them." According to Lawley and Alexander, Lee believed that many of his minority students picked up on Lee's personal experience as a student in Seattle's inner-city public schools from the anecdotes he shared with them as both a teacher and sports coach. Lee allowed that serving as a positive role model might have encouraged his students to focus more in the classroom, and noted that he always "encouraged students to exhibit as much effort as possible."

Middle school teacher Mick Denby observed that many of his students—both male and female—had few stable relationships with men outside of school, so they benefitted from positive relationships with male teachers. Though he admitted that his boys often pushed him to the limit and found it hard to let go of conflicts, Denby also observed that they were the "first ones to want to hang out," work as his teacher assistant, ask him how to manage relations with peers, seek advice on how to tie a necktie, or simply hang out. He noticed that some of his students continued to seek his company even after passing his grade level. "For some of these kids, I'm the only stable male they know," he said.

Sixth grade teacher Danielle Kaplan recalled that journaling was an effective way to "get at those kids with whom it was harder to make connections because they don't want to talk." Kaplan asked students to write daily journal entries in which they were to draw connections between their personal lives and whatever topic they were studying, believing this to be a "really great way to find out what's going on in their lives." "It's amazing what they'll write," she said. "They'll tell you a lot." Kaplan wrote back to each student in the journals in an effort to build a sense of family and community. She believed that connecting with students in this way allowed her to more equitably respond to their needs. "One-on-one time is limited," she said. "Often it's just to tell kids what they didn't do. To make up for the limited one-on-one time, I have to write back to them in their journals. It's a love-hate thing because of the amount of time it takes, but I lose touch without it."

Humor, Ethics, and Affirmations

According to Mick Denby, humor was integral to his efforts to "create a climate that is inviting and caring." He recalled that if something cracked him up, he'd share it with the class. Middle school principal Alicia Baldwin noted that the students in Kevin Friedman's classroom experienced a climate dramatically more positive than any they'd previously known. In her estimation, few teachers could keep up the steady stream of positive words that students heard daily from Friedman. He "is a master at making kids feel really good," said Baldwin. "It's just a natural part of who he is. He is there saying 'Hello' when the kids enter. You go into his classroom and it is upbeat: the comments, the constant affirmations. It's jovial. There's a lot of humor. It's quite amazing."

Three of the PTP administrators attributed the success of several male teachers to their even-tempered personalities and low-key style. Middle school principal Sela Hadžić recalled that students found teacher Charles Ackerman easy to talk to because they felt comfortable with him. Because he had good rapport and a personal relationship with students, the "kids loved him." Hadžić noted that Ackerman based his interactions with students on the principles of civility, patience, and support, and that he maintained a "low-key style . . . he spoke quietly and didn't yell or raise his voice."

Middle school teacher David Lee was also known for his even temperament. His principal, Bridget Lawley, noticed that he was welcoming, consistent, and clear, and that he didn't get upset with kids. She also noted that although he talked sternly he hardly ever raised his voice. Lee made students feel part of a group, and headed off potential problems to such an extent so that he never made discipline referrals. Lee himself stressed the importance of balancing hard work with extracurricular activities such as sports, music, dance, or drama. He worked to scaffold learning activities to "minimize the frustration level as much as possible," while giving students "constant reminders that they needed the occasional release of structured downtime."

Third grade teacher Ryan Toth and middle school teacher Kevin Friedman recognized students' efforts by awarding them points for completed work that entitled them to enter auctions for treats, extra school supplies, and games. "They love it," said Toth. "They tell me all the time that it's one of the things they really enjoy."

Connecting by Sharing Personal Experiences

Middle school teacher Angela Chaffee observed that her students "really like knowing about" her. One of the most powerful strategies she employed, particularly with black students, was letting them know about herself and elements of her personal life; she even kept a picture on her classroom wall of herself in 6th grade. As she put it, "telling kids about yourself helps you seem not so inhuman to them." Elementary school principal Rosalie de la Cruz noted that 4th grade teacher Mark Donnelly connected with students by sharing "a lot of personal experiences. They know when his baby was born, his kids' names—when he was remodeling his house, they knew about it. He even had students complete a WASL-type task on building a fence at the same time that he was building a fence at his new house." De la Cruz found that Donnelly and other strong teachers at her school continually personalized their classes as a way to provide cognitive scaffolding between prior learning and new content.

Elementary school principal Shannon Weller singled out 3rd grade teacher Donna Schneider for showing students that she "cared about students and their families" by opening up about her own hobbies. (One day she even brought her kayak to class and showed kids how to use it.) Another elementary school principal, Owen Callahan, made a similar observation about 3rd grade teacher Jeffrey Brooks, whose efforts to establish relationships with students, Callahan claimed, worked "especially well with black students." Brooks took the time to learn about his students, their interests, and their families through a survey that he had them complete; in addition, he shared information about himself with students, to demonstrate that "he was not an adversary." As a result of these efforts, students liked and respected Brooks, and felt that "he was there for them."

Extending Relationships, Support, and Caring Beyond the Classroom

Teachers and principals alike described several teachers as what Kleinfield (cited in Gay, 2000, p. 50) calls "warm demanders"—those who extend their relationship with and caring for students beyond the classroom while also holding them to high academic standards. Nearly 85 percent of the PTP educators went out of their way to provide students with after-school learning assistance; showed

caring by assisting them with personal needs; made home visits; and provided extra tutoring, lunchtime counseling sessions, or pep talks. For example, Kevin Friedman opened his doors to students prior to the beginning of class and after school, four days a week. David Lee went so far as to make himself available to all students and their parents or guardians at all times by cell phone.

Middle school principal Alicia Baldwin noted that teacher Marian Katz's support of her students even included financial assistance—"donating money to her students, or buying shoes for kids who don't have them. She has gone on her own and bought beauty supplies for the girls. She's paid them to work as teaching assistants so that they can earn the cash they need for necessities." When told that this behavior was quite unusual, Baldwin responded that PTP teachers were "real people who wanted to make a difference, no matter how weird it seemed to others."

Fairness, Respect, and Low Favoritism

Teacher-student social interactions in effective and culturally responsive classrooms are fair and mutually respectful, with teachers demonstrating care and interest in students' cultural and linguistic backgrounds and personal and academic growth (Arroyo, Rhoad, & Drew, 1999; Glasser, 1994; Knapp & Turnbull, 1991). These classrooms feature high social interaction (Delpit, 2000), low friction, and high levels of civility, with teachers and students alike demonstrating a commitment to democracy, civility, optimism, and a sense of family and community (Cummins, 1989; Garcia, 1991; Irvine & Armento, 2001). Irvine and Armento (2001) additionally found that all students in such classrooms are treated equally well and provided with equitable access to resources and opportunities to learn.

Like many PTP educators, middle school teacher Moira Reynolds established respect for every person as the paramount rule in her classroom. "Right off the bat, we talk a lot about respect and what's acceptable," she said. Reynolds believed that one of her most important tasks in building a climate of support for black students was "building a safe environment so that kids can talk and share ideas." Social interactions based on principles of human dignity contributed to a climate that promoted cohesiveness and collaborative learning. Middle school teacher Carla Storey also required her students to always be civil and respectful. "For instance, they can't say 'Shut up' to anyone in class," she said. "It's not civil behavior."

Sixth grade teacher Danielle Kaplan modeled and insisted on respect, at least in the classroom, from the beginning of the school year. She conceded that although she couldn't "say it was done in the halls," she worked to instill principles of human dignity among her students in the classroom. She listed her expectations: "We treat people with patience and respect, there's no interrupting, we talk in a respectful tone, and no one insults or puts down another." To help students learn expectations and internalize behavior management techniques, Kaplan commended or rewarded them when they abided by her rules, and took away privileges when they didn't. "I insist on being respectful," she said. "I'm firm and strict in modeling these expectations, because it is about human dignity; it's just human nature. People want to be treated with respect." She observed that 6th graders' "egos are sensitive. I talk to all students as intelligent people. I give them all responsibility for their learning. I want them to see that's how I see them."

According to David Lee and 3rd grade teacher Mark Goldberg, interactions grounded in fairness and consistency created an environment that bred success for black students. Goldberg said that he tried to "ensure that each child knows the value of every other child." He thought it was important to promote acceptance so that "no one feels that they are less or more than anybody else." In his view, treating everyone "according to who they are as individuals" allowed him to focus instruction on "moving forward based on individual skills and needs." Lee saw a need for equitable treatment because, prior to entering "Lee-land" (his name for his classroom), he believed that his students had too often been punished by teachers. Lee said that he "tried to be as consistent as possible in clearly presenting expectations so that students succeed." "When effort is present," he continued, "encouragement is often the route I select. But I am prepared to discipline when I feel it is necessary. If students feel there is fairness to how the classroom operates, that there are resources available to aid them, and that there are consistent rewards and consequences for both actions and inactions, those conditions breed success."

Promoting Student Interactions through Modeling

Principal de la Cruz has had to resolve instances when a personal connection and sense of fairness were not present in the classroom. "Sometimes, when you pull kids aside to discuss a problem and ask them what it's like in the teacher's classroom, we have this revelation as the kid says, 'The teacher never looks at me' or 'I raise my hand, but I never get picked,'" she said. Such students are able to discern fundamental disparities in their interactions with teachers and other students and to see a need for fairness and respect. "Kids have this justice scale of how things should be," said de la Cruz. "They are good at detecting when that is going on." She went on to praise 4th grade teacher Brian Gaynor for doing a "good job of modeling" the fairness and respect that he wanted his students to demonstrate, showing them "how he wants them to be."

"Fairness is a huge issue," said 3rd grade teacher Kimberly Lazarides. "I've noticed that if students don't think that they're being treated fairly—for instance, if I say one person can go to the bathroom, while another one can't—that really affects them. I've learned that to preserve the relationship I have with students, I must treat them all equally well. They really need to know that things are fair and that I'm treating everybody the same."

Angela Chaffee argued that one of the ways to help students learn to treat each other more humanely was for teachers to demonstrate their humanity to students. Like Lazarides, she found this strategy effective with all her students, regardless of race. Letting

students know that teachers made mistakes helped students see "that it's okay to make mistakes."

Alicia Baldwin and Berkeley McGuire identified how various aspects of McGuire's interactions with students promoted fairness, respect, and low favoritism. For example, Baldwin noticed that McGuire tended to dress well, and in so doing exhibited respect for her students. "I think if you are respectful to your students and show that teaching is an important job for you, that's an important statement," said Baldwin. McGuire considered the nuances of both her verbal and nonverbal communication style. "If I'm not inviting in my voice and body, if I'm mean-spirited but not firm, it will turn students off," she said. "Students know when I'm firm, fair, and consistent. They would notice it if I were not. They know it and they respond by owning up to their poor choices."

Promoting Student Interactions through Purposeful Instruction

To promote interactions based on the principles of human dignity, democracy, equity, and justice, Kimberly Lazarides found that it helps to devote time each year to teaching character education. "We talk and read about concepts such as friendship, respect, and honesty throughout the year to help students understand, develop, and internalize guidelines for classroom behavior," she said. "In addition, our counselor conducts an anti-bullying program for students."

PTP teachers found that sharing power and decision making with students was an effective motivational strategy that also conveyed fairness and respect. Angela Chaffee maintained that she changed the power relationship in her classroom when she invited students to ask questions and give her feedback on the effectiveness of her lessons. Although she accepted that she was the adult in the classroom, she wanted to develop a level of mutual respect with her students. "I want kids to know that I'm not perfect—I'm human," she said.

Principal Bridget Lawley held teacher Susan Lansing's class up as a good example of one in which students and teacher shared power. Lansing, she said, "accepted multiple responses, acknowledged more than one solution, and didn't have to be the one to provide the correct answer." Lawley noted that Lansing "encouraged individual thinking and diversity of thinking" by encouraging students to demonstrate learning in a variety of ways, with some students writing or orally discussing ideas while others critiqued and verified the correctness of solutions.

Alicia Baldwin suggested that teacher Gillian Novak's role as a parent outside of school helped her to embrace and promote democratic principles in class. "I see a difference when people have had kids," she said. "It's so theoretical until you have raised kids. I think Gillian, as an older teacher in a second career, tends to integrate more democratic principles in her teaching, because she treats children the way she would want other people to treat her own."

Low Friction

Principal Alex La Chuisa noticed that a sarcastic or confrontational approach to students was counterproductive, especially with black boys. He found that teachers become "less and less confrontational the longer that they teach kids of color." Middle school teacher Gillian Novak tried "not to be confrontational" and to show respect for alternative opinions. "I try to build relations and understand where students are coming from," she said. Angela Chaffee allowed that her responses to students varied according to their backgrounds and their academic and interpersonal needs. "If I know that to be confrontational with a student will cause him to react in a negative way, I'm not going to do it," she said. "From what I have seen, this is more an issue with black boys than girls."

Middle school teacher Mick Denby found that creating a sense of family in his classroom helped to reduce friction. "I have a rule: 'What happens here, stays here,'" he said. "It's a family thing."

Conclusion

PTP educators promoted caring, fair, respectful, and equitable social and academic interactions in their classrooms in a variety of ways. Kimberly Lazarides chose to teach character education and demonstrated unflagging "patience and kindness" in the process, according to principal Erdie Baptiste. Teachers Carla Storey, Diana Granger, and Adrianne Driscoll shaped interactions in their schools to counter the negative treatment that they had seen people of color habitually subjected to outside school. David Maslin brought issues of oppression to the forefront through classroom discussions and by changing the power relationships with students. David Lee crafted responses to his students that reflected lessons he learned growing up in multicultural Seattle. Jeffrey Brooks pointed out how ostensibly equitable disciplinary practices can hinder minority students if they are not informed by an understanding of accepted norms of behavior among diverse cultural groups.

PTP educators not only treated their students with civility, patience, and support but also worked purposefully to ensure that students of color or living in poverty weren't singled out, oppressed, or treated inequitably. Through their efforts, PTP educators were able to create positive contexts for both interpersonal relations and learning activities—classrooms alive with discussion, problem solving, and learning, and marked by low friction as well.

3

Classroom Climate

In this chapter, we will examine how the PTP educators implemented the following strategies:

Category: Cohesiveness

Strategies: Teachers . . .

- Promote a group-centered, collaborative approach to learning.
- Promote a positive, familial classroom climate.
- Group students according to shared traits to stimulate enjoyment and cohesiveness.
- Identify and counteract stereotypes by teaching students about universal traits and values.
- Understand that classroom instruction reflects elements of both the community and school.
- Involve family and community in students' learning.
- Create positive relationships and collaborate meaningfully with parents and community members to further the educational development of students.

Category: Low Apathy

Strategies: Teachers . . .

- Foster both student and teacher interest in teaching and learning.

- Arouse student curiosity and explain the purpose and practical application of content.
- Promote student interest in what goes on in class.

Category: Productive Learning Environments
Strategies: Teachers . . .
- Maintain a safe and orderly classroom.
- Balance established routines and rituals with excitement.
- Establish a physically inviting classroom.
- Understand that the classroom climate reflects elements of both the community and school.

Cohesiveness

Middle school principal Alicia Baldwin described teacher Kevin Friedman's classroom environment as uniquely strong and cohesive. Friedman's blend of affirmations, humor, and support encouraged students to work together to help each other learn. "It's almost as if learning about social interactions was an academic pursuit" for Friedman, said Baldwin.

Fourth grade teacher Diana Granger also focused largely on social interactions in her classroom. According to Granger, she and the other teachers at her school complemented their efforts to build relationships with students with efforts to teach students how to build relationships with each other. The resultant community environment contributed to a climate that educators felt was conducive to cooperative learning. Granger recalled that she and her colleagues wanted their students to feel "like they were coming home to a place of their own—a second home." To this end, they ensured that their classrooms were physically inviting—"bright and engaging spaces where students can use manipulatives, touch things with their hands, and manipulate the environment."

Elementary school principal Darrell Conway felt that Granger was particularly successful at developing "an inclusive classroom environment that allowed students to use their differences to their advantage." She coached students to reflect on and critique their thoughts, feelings, and behaviors when they were not getting along with each other. According to Granger, such coaching "allows teachers to build relationships with children, and students to build relationships with each other so that they trust each other in their learning."

Promoting trust among students figured significantly in middle school teacher Gillian Novak's efforts to develop familial relationships in her class. "My first goal is developing a sense of community, family, and caring," she said. "I have students work together in small groups—and to form the groups themselves—so that they learn to trust each other." For Novak, the goal of classroom interactions was to instill in students the principles of support, respect, and optimism.

Promoting a Positive, Familial Climate

Teacher Adrianne Driscoll looks into her students' backgrounds and uses what she learns to create a familial climate and community of trust in her classroom. "I think this is a very important strategy," she said. "A lot of the kids we get aren't getting the support they need at home. Some have been in more than one foster home this year, or their families are homeless. They've got to get the nurturing somewhere. We're like home to a lot of the kids." At Driscoll's school, which had a 90 percent black student population, teachers worked hard to help their black students build a sense of ethnic identity. Every teacher at the school chose a country in Africa on which to focus, allowing students to explore cultural differences and learn about similarities between their own lives and those of African children. Teachers were also encouraged to display pennants for historically black colleges or universities in their classrooms, to convey the message that a college future was out there for students.

Middle school teacher Berkeley McGuire thought that having students for three periods in a block schedule allowed her more time to establish a relationship with each student. She said that her students were aware of her commitment to them and knew that she "took personal responsibility for them." "I considered them 'my children,'" she said. "If another kid was bothering them, they knew I'd protect them." However, because her students showed that they cared about each other, McGuire had few problems. She recalled telling students, "It's important that you get along. I'm going to teach you how to get along with each other." On the rare occasions when tensions arose, she did not immediately change students' seating arrangements, but rather taught behaviors that led to smoother interactions, such as how to apologize and how to communicate appropriately through body language.

Several PTP teachers used class meetings as a way to build a sense of family and community among their students. For instance, elementary school principal Shannon Weller noted that 3rd grade teacher Donna Schneider's class was "a very positive environment for the kids, featuring wonderful class meetings where kids shared social issues and validated each other's input." At the Marcus Garvey Academy, all of the school's 48 6th graders came together for daily meetings in which students shared concerns and aired grievances while teachers coached them on appropriate behavior. To encourage cohesion and a familial climate, teachers and students often repeated the following chant: "We are the 6th grade, and we're going to represent!"

Building Positive Relations and Meaningful Collaboration with Parents or Guardians

PTP educators took care to form meaningful relationships with parents and other caregivers, ensuring that they were involved and held valued roles in the life of the school. According to Arroyo, Rhoad, and Drew (1999), parents do well to serve as knowledgeable advocates for realistic academic expectations among students and teachers. In addition, they can help teachers understand students' strengths, concerns, and growth areas, and share their talents and skills within the context of school governance. PTP educators collaborated with parents and caregivers both on school activities and as volunteers in community-based organizations to help students develop academically, socially, and emotionally. The teachers with whom I spoke highlighted the following six types of collaborative activities and behaviors that they believed were essential to the success of teacher-parent partnerships:

1. Establishing purposeful, clear, frequent, two-way positive communication between teachers and parents or caregivers regarding school programs, learning and assessment activities, and student progress toward learning goals. This type of communication motivates parents to share their concerns about school with students, help students with learning tasks, and monitor students' school progress. Elementary school principal Rosalie de la Cruz noted that, at her school, "teachers start making connections with families early in the year" to develop positive relations and meaningful collaboration. Mark Donnelly, a 4th grade teacher at de la Cruz's school, said he used the Open House meetings at the start of the school year to initiate meaningful collaboration with parents and involve them substantively in their children's school life. "At Open House, I set apart time to say to parents, 'Here's what I do, and here's what you can do to help,'" he said.

Elementary school principal Joanne Stewart characterized 3rd grade teacher Mark Goldberg's contacts with parents and caregivers as frequent, substantive, and focused on making connections and solving problems. "If a child has a problem, he picks up the phone and calls parents," said Stewart. "There is an emphasis on connections with families." Adrianne Driscoll said that she tried to talk to parents as often as possible, emphasizing that she saw herself as a "cheerleader" for her

students—"the person who is in their corner saying, 'Isn't this kid great?'" Because many of her students came from difficult backgrounds, Driscoll felt it was important to share her belief in their capacity to achieve: "A lot of these kids need all the boosts they can get, especially the ones in foster care, in one home after another."

According to middle school teacher Moira Reynolds, "being in very close contact with parents has always been a saving grace. I'm always emailing or calling them, whether it's good news or bad news. I try to make a point of calling parents when a student has improved."

2. Mitigating the discontinuity between home and school by honoring the values, cultures, and languages of students' home communities and the families' capacity to contribute substantively to students' success. "I have great, meaningful relationships with parents," said 4th grade teacher Chloe Gifford. "And parents are very supportive when I get on the phone right away about kids who are disrespectful or having problems learning. And because of what I do, although I'm white and the kids are black, I don't have the problem of parents saying that I have treated anybody differently or that students all needed to be treated equally well."

Elementary school principal Tate Fisher noted that 4th grade teacher Christie Wyatt also had a positive relationship with parents. "As a white teacher, she communicates effectively with students and parents of all cultural and ethnic groups," said Fisher. "I work hard to break down stereotypes," said Wyatt. "One mother was clear that she wanted to trust me, but wanted to know if a white teacher could treat her black kid right. It's not just black folks, but minorities in general. They want to have dialogue, but there's a little distrust of the educational system. Lots of parents are afraid of school and don't want to have anything to do with teachers. I know that sometimes a teacher's personality can impede progress with some parents. And just as parents are anxious, teachers are anxious too: white teachers will often quickly talk to white parents, but fear black parents. I've come to the conclusion that some white teachers are even afraid of black parents. I am not worried about the parents getting mad, insulting me, or yelling at me. There's an art to talking to parents. First, I try to put them at ease. Second, I let them talk to me so that they can relax during and at the end of the dialogue. Third and most important, I acknowledge what they say, and ask them to think about what I have said." For collaborations with parents to work, Wyatt offered, "I think you just have to say, 'Look at a child as a child.' For example, I ask parents, 'What do you expect for your child?' I believe that, 95 percent of the time, parents are right about their kids."

3. Learning about the traits and needs of all students and their families and recognizing that students' families know the most about them and therefore have much to offer. Fourth grade teacher Christie Wyatt went through her students' school folders to learn about their strengths and weaknesses, listened closely to what students said about themselves and their homes, and helped students understand their individual roles in mastering content. "I map each kid's skills as high, medium, or low and share the results with parents," she said. Wyatt forms a rapport with students' parents as early as possible to establish educational goals and secure families' support in developing learning plans.

4. Creating and maintaining open and caring parent-school relationships and welcoming climates that are supportive of students' educational careers. According to elementary school principal Mai Pham, getting to know students' families absolutely influenced the students' success. "I know every child and most students' parents by name," she said. "As a person of color, I can relate to parents and kids. They will not scream at me about discrimination because they know that I love their kids and I go to their homes." Pham emphasized that she and 3rd grade teacher Glen Roberts were able to develop positive and meaningful collaboration with parents because their relationships were based on human dignity principles of trust and honesty. "Parents here feel well informed about their kids," she said.

Elementary school principal Joanne Stewart noted that 3rd grade teacher Mark Goldberg demonstrated honesty and trust to parents by endeavoring to always be consistent. "More than anything else, Mark worked on consistency," she said. "The parents of our students demanded that all students be treated equally well."

5. Sharing responsibility when helping students complete learning activities

outside the classroom. Third grade teacher Ryan Toth engaged parents in helping children practice for the district's Direct Writing Assessment. According to Toth, many 3rd grade students were "overwhelmed at the beginning of the year, so we really worked hard to teach the writing process" and show parents how to help students with a weekly home writing assignment. "I talk to them at Open House, and in my newsletter I send home ideas for working with their children on writing," he said. "I really attribute a lot of our success on the assessments this year to my parents' input. I'm happy I'm at a school where there's great input from the parents and we can hold the kids accountable at both ends."

6. Changing internal and external structures that create opportunities for parents and community members to partner and participate productively in school. The educators at Toth's school made an effort to actively involve parents in teaching and learning, particularly through the school's highly esteemed reading and literacy program. Toth felt that because the adults working in the Read Naturally program were highly trained, their contributions were particularly substantive. "The parents who come to volunteer usually stay on," he said. "They love it because they get such positive feedback. And I feel very lucky because I have the parents here as a resource."

Toth noted that educators in his school created and maintained an open and welcoming climate in which parents directly supported teachers. He contacted parents during the first week of school to share the positive attributes he saw in individual students and let parents know that he welcomed their participation in his classroom. He told parents that his biweekly newsletter would be their conduit for staying informed about what was going on in the classroom. "I tell parents out front: 'I don't want anybody coming in and sitting and watching,'" he said. "They're entitled to do that the first time, but after that, I really want them involved with the kids. Sometimes they'll sit and correct papers or go out on field trips, but mostly they worked with small groups." Toth believed that parental involvement in the classroom was "a big factor" in his students' achievement.

Low Apathy

In PTP educators' classrooms, teachers function as cheerleaders, supporting students' motivation to engage in and achieve learning goals. Fourth grade teacher Chloe Gifford shared how she conveyed her passion for learning to her students: "In mathematics, I'm passionate. I mean, I love to teach reading, that's fun, but I'm *really* passionate about mathematics. That's my love. For the kids, I find that it becomes *their* love, too, because I just cannot help but to pass it on." Principal Patrice Tam thought that Gifford created "a fun classroom" by being "vibrant, enthusiastic, and thoroughly enjoying what she is doing."

Middle school teacher Angela Chaffee also set the goal of getting her students excited about learning. She believed that her own excitement about learning was infectious and would eventually lead her students to develop a love of learning. She recalled seeing students start smiling as she presented a lesson, and she found that piquing their interest was "pretty powerful for them because at some point they wouldn't be sitting in a classroom." Getting students excited about learning in middle school, she felt, meant getting them to love learning for life.

Many PTP educators emphasized the importance of the learning space to the effectiveness of their students' community building and cooperative learning activities. Fourth grade teacher Diana Granger stated she and her teaching partners created a "bright, engaging, inviting environment in which kids could touch and manipulate items with their hands." Students helped to create just such an environment by deciding what art to hang, whether to erect a train set, and other ways to demonstrate their interests in the classroom. Granger said that her students ultimately chose to place the classroom's 10 computers in a bank along the hallway due to the limited working space in the classroom. As she put it, the students' decision making "helped to create the community."

According to elementary school principal Rosalie de la Cruz, 4th grade teacher Mark Donnelly's ability to "mellow out" students who had trouble in other settings was one of his most effective traits. He accomplished this in part by creating an inviting, familial environment that reflected, in a number of ways, personal caring for students. His classroom was physically inviting: "Not Spartan, but without a lot of stuff and clutter," said de la Cruz. "He has a fish tank and a couch for reading." More

importantly, Donnelly treated students with civility, patience, and support. "That is his greatest strength," said de la Cruz. "When he lectures, he has the kids gather around him on the rug on the floor. He makes a point of being on the same level as they are, just like teachers do with younger kids."

In Chloe Gifford's class, students took responsibility for maintaining an appropriate social climate and physical environment. She recalled that students took their roles seriously, at one point asking to reorganize the library, which she had inherited from the teacher who had previously been assigned to her room. The students declared that they thought alphabetizing books by title made more sense than doing so by author, which Gifford thought was a fine idea.

Productive Learning Environments

PTP educators emphasized the importance of physically and emotionally safe learning environments. Third grade teacher Kimberly Lazarides and middle school teacher Jessica Wakefield both worked to establish safe classrooms because they believed that students craved the structure and rules that prevented interactions from becoming chaotic. For middle school teachers Moira Reynolds and Michael Wagner, maintaining a level of comfort in their classrooms was one prerequisite for students to feel open to communicating ideas and participating in learning activities. Wagner felt strongly that the expectations for everyone to participate had to be balanced by an understanding that such participation is emotionally safe. "I communicate to the kids that no one will laugh, and no one will criticize," he said.

Middle school teacher Lisa Forsythe stressed that she was "consistent and pretty strict about expectations for respect." As an example, she noted that students in her class were required to "sit up, not flop over" when she or other students talked. She believed that this kind of respectful attention was "appreciated in the end, because the students then have an environment that is conducive to learning; behavior is controlled and well-managed." Bridget Lawley, the principal at Forsythe's school, noted that the orderliness Forsythe created by having students sit in rows was nicely balanced by allowing students freedom of choice in other areas. For instance, during a walk through Forsythe's social studies class, students were advised to make themselves comfortable sitting in chairs or on the floor while they completed a group pretest on the unit on Africa. As Forsythe leads a discussion during which students validate the reasons for their choices on the answers to items in the pretest, she encourages students to value discourse, respect varying opinions, and present their personal, cultural, or text-based perspectives on the test items.

When Lawley spoke of teacher David Lee's classroom, she enthused about the number of ways he brought order to it and showed his concern for students and their workspace. For instance, to reduce noise levels when his students moved chairs from rows to groups of four, he put felt tips on chair legs. He also cleaned and repaired tabletops and desks in his classroom, and had teaching assistants help him keep up with data entry on students' daily work, organize and prepare teaching materials and files, and make bulletin boards. Commending him as someone who "used teaching assistants more efficiently than anyone I know," Lawley noted that students vied to be his assistants. The extent to which Lee had taught students his methods for maintaining order in the classroom was demonstrated one afternoon when a student who had forgotten her homework escorted Lawley into the classroom and quickly found the needed books, materials, and assignment planner.

Once students internalize a sense of pride in their surroundings, they do not need to be constantly reminded to keep the classroom in order. "I don't have to say, 'In order to make a safe, orderly and pleasant classroom, let's do this,'" said Chloe Gifford. "Students do it themselves. They're pretty good about keeping the room cleaned up." To help maintain order, Gifford assigned roles and tasks commonly delegated in classrooms using cooperative group instruction. For instance, to help groups accomplish tasks and to make learning activities run smoothly, students assumed responsibility for "picking up and passing out the materials, confirming directions, or presenting orally to the class."

Routines and Rituals that Contribute to Safe and Orderly Classrooms

According to several PTP educators, the presence of classroom routines that the students knew and could count on was an important factor in student achievement. "I know that some students have very challenging backgrounds and home lives fraught with many surprises," said middle school teacher

Chris Spelman. "For them, having a structure at school and things that they can count on, that aren't surprises, is reassuring. . . . For a lot of students, just having a structure—knowing, for example, that on Monday we're going to start off with journaling and then work into weekly vocabulary—for the kids, there's more safety. That's not to say I don't push them academically, because I do. But they know and I know that I have a set of routines that we follow."

PTP educators' management methods were characterized by consistency, explicit explanations of rules and consequences, firmness in follow-through, and fun modeling of expectations. Like most PTP educators, Spelman spent time at the beginning of the year creating an orderly environment by making classroom rules and expectations explicit, and then reviewed expectations often throughout the year to make sure that his students understood them. Middle school teacher Jessica Wakefield also began every year by providing explicit coaching on appropriate behavior and ensuring that her students knew her expectations for classroom routines. Likewise, at the beginning of the year, teacher Adrianne Driscoll made explicit her rules and expectations and provided explicit coaching on appropriate behavior through role plays. Driscoll found that "if you have specific procedures for things and can refer back to them every few weeks, when students forget, things tend to go smoothly."

David Lee reinforced understandings of procedures in his classroom that were instilled through multiple repetitions by also having students map out upcoming events in their planners, and Jessica Wakefield actively taught students how to use tools such as assignment sheets to organize task completion expectations. Beginning the year in much the same way, Lisa Forsythe taught lessons about her expectations and the procedures and structures of her classroom, such as how to move desks into twos, into fours, and then back into rows; where to find supplies; and where to place history books. At the same time, Forsythe was fond of implementing "fun and surprise activities on certain days, so that students don't know what's going to happen until they come to class."

Balancing Rituals and Routines with Excitement

"I want to do things in ways that are interesting and unique," noted 3rd grade teacher Glen Roberts. He emphasized that he wanted his "presentations to show a sense of personality, not to be dry." In order to add some levity to his lessons, he said that he had begun to "investigate how to do different faces" for students. Fourth grade teacher Jeffrey Brooks noted that "as a teacher, you have to be a little bit of a ham. You've got to be just entertaining enough for students to be interested in the lesson, but not distracted."

Middle school teacher Susan Lansing used a strategy promoted by the National Urban Alliance called "dancing definitions," in which teachers and students set lyrics that contain important information about a topic to rhythmic music, as a way to reinforce learning of geometry concepts. She lamented not having learned about dancing definitions years ago. "Now everybody in the district is doing it," she said. "The teacher is up there acting like a fool. Students are laughing, enjoying it. Some students really don't like the math algorithms that are just drill and practice."

Establishing a Safe and Physically Inviting Classroom

Diana Granger and her team teacher began every year by asking themselves how best to make their classrooms warm and inviting. "We really stress that idea that this is the students' second home," she said. "We want to make the environment reflect that." To that end, Granger's classroom featured a fish tank, a reading area with a sofa, a train set, banks of computers both inside the classroom and in the hallway, a fishing boat propped against the wall in the hallway, and large windows with views of the Cascade Mountains and Puget Sound. "We really wanted to access that view," said Granger. "For next year, we already have some ideas about building a long worktable up against the window so kids can study and look out at the mountains and Puget Sound. Since our big idea over the next two years is stewardship, we really want students to be connected to their environment."

Jeffrey Brooks noted that his school team actively attempted to create a positive, comfortable, familial climate for students, pointing specifically to the school's open concept floorplan, which was designed to encourage collaboration, innovation, and flexibility, and to the couch in his classroom, which gave the space a homey atmosphere. Middle school principal Alicia Baldwin noted that teacher Marian Katz also created a warm environment through the use of beanbags. "I particularly noticed young black boys leaving their desks to go sit in beanbags and cuddle up next to each other and read," she said. "They're very comfortable. These are middle school boys who might not read otherwise."

Adrianne Driscoll emphasized the importance of culturally relevant decorations in the classroom. "I make sure that I not only have math manipulatives and visual displays of mathematical concepts, but also artifacts that my brother and other travelers have brought back from Africa," she said. Her class is filled with artifacts, posters, books, and pictures related to Africa and great African and African American leaders.

4

Classroom Management

In this chapter, we will examine how the PTP educators implemented the following strategies:

Teachers . . .
- Use appropriate language.
- Discipline using an adult voice.
- Temper order and established standards with equal parts respect—are caring, yet firm.
- Prevent situations where students lose peer respect.
- Respond to misbehavior on an individual basis.
- Match discipline to students' home culture and language.
- Provide explicit coaching on appropriate behavior.
- Explicitly communicate their expectations of students' roles and behaviors.
- Teach mediation and coping skills.

Classroom management is integral to the success of teaching and learning in the classrooms of effective and culturally responsive teachers. As the previous chapters in this book have shown, PTP educators followed an ethic of caring that helped students see what was truly valued in classrooms and schools. Teachers continually tempered activities to preserve order and established standards with excitement and authentic displays of respect and care.

In addition, when students saw how teachers and administrators handled difficulties that arose with their classmates, they learned how they themselves might be treated in similar situations.

Sixth grade teacher Danielle Kaplan stressed the need to not single out and disproportionately discipline black students in class, particularly as they are too often subjected to such dynamics outside of school. For his part, middle school teacher David Maslin explicitly discussed such dynamics, which he characterized as oppressive, with students when establishing the norms and expectations for interpersonal interactions in his classroom.

For 4th grade teacher Diana Granger, "classroom management goes back to the idea of community." Her teaching team used daily community circle meetings to "celebrate learning, discuss decisions we have to make, problem solve," and teach students how to interact with each other in ways that preserved a sense of community in the classroom. "We began the year with the goals of promoting democratic interactions in the classroom and with the idea that the adults aren't here to box in and control students' ideas and actions." In addition, Granger used a piece of culturally relevant literature—Toni Morrison's first children's book, *The Big Box*—to begin discussions about the etiquette, rules, and expectations of the classroom. The book presents a critical view of adult-child relationships in the United States, questioning the ways in which adults might hinder the development of a child's creativity and independence through the imposition of structures, rules, and values. Granger used themes from the book to help students consider the meanings of freedom and responsibility among both adults and students. As Granger and her team read the book, they spent a few weeks discussing the idea that freedom requires responsibility and specifically defining what this idea means in the classroom. To help students critique the book's teachings about freedom, adults on Granger's team posed questions such as "Is it freedom if I want to run all over the classroom and run into somebody?" and "If freedom is doing whatever I want to do, is that okay?" In response to such questions, students arrived at the conclusion that an individual's freedom should not infringe upon the freedom of others. Granger felt that this was "a huge idea for the kids, and one on which we could base our behavior in class." The result of students' and teachers' problem solving was a team agreement that hung in the hallway, where everyone could refer to it. From time to time, Granger said, she and her team discussed and revised what they called the "living document which represents us and which we all signed."

Teaching students to examine, manage, and understand the motivation behind their behaviors was integral to Granger's team, and she believed that community-building efforts helped staff to establish the relationships with students necessary for doing so. "We can sit down and say to a student, 'I noticed that you have a kind of grumpy voice with your friends this morning, and I'm just wondering, how are you feeling this morning? What's going on?'" Granger said. "Because we connect with the kids, we can sit down and have that conversation. And the conversation does not sound like: 'You said "Shut up" three times; go to the office.' That approach just doesn't address the child's social and emotional growth."

If Granger and her team partner saw several students engaging in "behavior that kind of aggravated others: a lot of touching, name calling, or generally just getting on each other's nerves," they addressed the behavior in a community circle, where they asked students to "focus inward and reflect on their own behavior" through probing questions (e.g., "Why do you think we're behaving that way?"). Through this type of questioning, Granger believed that teachers led students to consider engaging in behaviors that supported the team agreement. Group reflection sessions also promoted a sense of collectiveness and collaboration and self-efficacy development.

Positive student-teacher relationships are the foundation of David Maslin's classroom management approach. "My classroom has many styles—for better or worse," he said. "There's a mix of preadolescent and adolescent attitudes. . . . Because disruptive behavior disrupts learning for all of us, I keep group discussions as positive as possible. I can't control every contingency, but I've found that there are certain ways to react when someone disrupts." When Maslin's principal, Tom McFadden, reflected on his classroom management style, he noted that Maslin was "not nasty or demeaning when calling kids on stuff." His classroom climate was characterized by a low degree of friction; everyone practiced civility, patience, and support.

According to principal Alex La Chuisa, the positive milieu that middle school teacher Angela Chaffee created in her classroom was essential to good classroom management. "She has a positive and caring personality that is the foundation for her positive relationships with students," said La Chuisa. "I

treat my students as I would treat my own kids," agreed Chaffee. Instead of developing consequences for "every imaginable infraction," Chaffee said that she grounded interactions in the human dignity principles of civility and support. "I try to develop a level of respect with all my kids," she said. "And if respect's there, generally, they don't want or tend to do things to disappoint you. Sometimes all it takes is a look to let them know you're disappointed or to get them to correct their own behavior."

Setting Expectations That Are Transparent, Consistent, and Responsive to Student Needs

"Both consistency and flexibility are important," said Chaffee. "I start off doing the same thing every year to see how kids are going to react. If my techniques don't work, that's where flexibility comes in—tweaking what needs to be tweaked." Her principal went even further: "When kids make a bad decision and Angela calls them on it, she also *counsels* them," said La Chuisa. "When she imposes consequences, she listens and gives strategies they can use to do better." La Chuisa also noted that Chaffee tried as much as possible to handle discipline concerns within her classroom. "Unless it's a big problem, I don't bring the parents or the administration in," affirmed Chaffee. "When I do that, I've lost control of the ability to manage, because I've given over my authority to other people."

Middle school teacher Moira Reynolds was also reluctant to refer students to school administration when they committed infractions, noting that she did not want to "put students into the system by developing a history of referrals to the office." Although she "definitely used administration for support and connected with parents," she found that "having students look at their behavior in terms of the class, and making appropriate consequences within the classroom instead of kind of shuffling them out to the other parts of the school" proved more effective.

Angela Chaffee believed that her students had aligned their motivation and actions with her behavior expectations because she was "transparent, reasonable, firm, and fair." She also worked to satisfy students' curiosity about the purpose of behavior guidelines and to help them understand their individual roles by asking a series of questions. "In the beginning of the year, I don't just say, 'These are the rules,'" she said. "I ask, 'Why do you think I value these rules? Why do you think this is important? If we didn't do this, how do you think things would work in the classroom?' As a result, they understand why I do things a certain way."

In Carla Storey's classroom, if students "do a good job managing their behavior, the whole class can participate in games on Friday." She also instituted a system that she called "Me and You Points." She explained: "If the kids follow the rules and expectations, they earn points. If they get three to five points daily for good behavior, they get cards redeemable for items at the school's Student Store. If they are out of line, I give myself points. If they get 10 points, we have games; if I get 10 points, there are no games on Friday."

Matching Discipline to Students' Home Culture and Language

Because Lisa Forsythe was familiar with her students' home lives and backgrounds, she felt comfortable "pulling kids aside, calling them on their behavior, and telling them, 'Look, that's not okay. It wouldn't be okay at home. So let's not do it here.' Or coaching them to understand, 'This is when that behavior is okay, but this is when it is not okay.'" Forsythe said that she has relied upon wisdom about "cultural norms learned from the community and the kind of school we are" to guide her in this area. "I think black parents have high expectations for their kids," she said. "And although every family has cultural differences and unique traits, I think that I'm just reinforcing what parents expect when I tell my students, 'Parents expect it. I expect it. This is how we do things.'"

Sixth grade teacher Danielle Kaplan championed the importance of "treating everyone with respect and being fair." Her knowledge of the modal beliefs and styles of interaction and communication common to black culture convinced her that "black kids are sensitive to being singled out, as well they should be. It's important not to spotlight kids. If I have to talk to them, I do so in private." She continued: "In middle school, black boys especially seem active and noisy. I talk to them in private and say, 'This is what I need. This is what you must do.' Their responses have been pretty positive."

Taking discussions of infractions to the hallway outside the classroom, having private conversations with students during lunch time, not singling out students for censure, and redirecting students' energies when they engage in disruptive behaviors are a few of the methods PTP teachers used to ensure that students were not embarrassed or insulted in the course of disciplinary actions. For example, middle school teacher Mick Denby regularly took disruptive students into the hall for conferences during which he modeled and explicitly coached the students on appropriate behavior.

Developing Self-Efficacy in Managing Behavior

Building self-efficacy is "all about the kids choosing to change their own behavior," said Angela Chaffee. "That's one thing about middle school: kids are starting to get out from underneath their parents' wings. I tell them they have a choice to do things differently; I'm not going to *make* them do anything. I tell them, 'This is about you. You can choose your behavior, and if you choose not to, then that's when I'll bring your parents in.' It's really powerful for them because they start to feel responsible."

Third grade teacher Ryan Toth instituted a clearly articulated system of consequences for disruptive behavior: a warning after the first disruption, writing names on the board after the second, and assigning 10 minutes of detention after the third. "Kids tend to understand the system right away," he said. To temper his desire for an orderly classroom with his respect for his students, and to give students a chance to demonstrate that they are making better decisions, Roth crossed any names

off the board four times a day. "It builds character to give students more chances," he said.

Toth's flexibility and belief in student decision making also led him to consider the importance of space when disciplining students, particularly since his classroom was in an outdoor portable unit: "If the weather was decent and the incident didn't warrant an immediate discussion, I'd let students hang outside for a little bit. I'd say privately, 'Wait here on the porch for two or three minutes, and when you're ready, come in.' I gave them space, distance, and time, and I let them save face if they had done something really embarrassing."

In addition to allowing students a physical respite from the classroom, Toth lent a caring ear to their concerns. "I try to listen and give students a voice," he said. "I will give them, and they know they will have, an opportunity to express whatever's bothering them. They know that there might be consequences, but they will also get a chance to vent and come to solutions. Often, they need to get things out of their system before they could focus in class." Although he made himself available to all students, Toth said it was most often boys who needed to vent, "because they are the ones who'll often come in fiery."

Toth also helped students channel their energy into positive outlets by enlisting them to tutor younger students in nearby classrooms or serve as buddies to special education students. "After giving them a chance to vent, I put them into service, working with someone unrelated to their problem or issue," he said. "It has helped children learn to channel that energy into something really positive rather than something negative. I believe in moving on and putting that energy somewhere else."

Reducing Discipline Problems Through Appropriate and Engaging Instruction

In her years working as an educator in Atlanta's predominantly black school district, Angela Chaffee learned that providing engaging, developmentally appropriate instruction reduced the likelihood of discipline problems. She also found that scaffolding learning activities to match her students' backgrounds and helping students to understand academic objectives proved helpful. "A lot of the time, what was being presented in the curriculum was so far over the kids' heads, they didn't know what to value," she said. "So to get them hooked, I would adjust the way I presented the information so that they could understand it. . . . If you're always teaching above somebody's head, if kids don't understand, you're going to have discipline problems."

Fourth grade teacher Jeffrey Brooks concurred with Chaffee's assessment. "We have usually found that we don't have management problems if kids are engaged in multiple meaningful ways," he said. "We concentrate on instruction, trying to make the learning as engaging and challenging as possible."

Explicitly Communicating Student Roles and Teacher Expectations

PTP teachers described the necessity of gaining personal clarity about expectations prior to being able to support students. "It's pretty critical for me to know ahead of time what

I want and to explain it explicitly so there's no confusion," said Moira Reynolds. "I think that a lot of behavior issues can come from students not being clear about what they are supposed to do at any given time." Mark Donnelly agreed. "By modeling and making the rules and behavioral expectations explicit," he said, "I gave kids responsibility" for managing their behavior and developing self-efficacy and self-control.

Third grade teacher Donna Schneider, who teaches in a Montessori program at one PTP school, noted that her "students are taught and internalize expectations early on, and are given clear boundaries and support for those boundaries." She noted that, in her school, teachers regularly demonstrated to students "how they should be engaged" and provided "encouragement for doing things the right way."

Adrianne Driscoll and her teaching partner sometimes used what they called "Think Time" to correct student misbehavior. If disruptive students didn't behave after being told to, Driscoll or her partner would send them to a neighboring classroom, where they were to reflect in writing on their inappropriate conduct and create a plan for how they will behave in the future before returning to class. "As soon as I have a moment, I look over what they've written," said Driscoll, "and I give them explicit coaching on appropriate behavior, saying, for instance, 'You know, you have this right. I agree with you.' Or 'Yes, but this is only part of it. There are still some things that you're doing that are making it hard for you to learn and for me to teach. Go back and keep thinking.' And they go back, and once they have it, I say, 'Okay, this is great.'" If what the students wrote still did not reflect an adequate understanding of expected behavior, Driscoll reserved the right to send the form home to the students' parents.

A Virtual Walk through Jeffrey Brooks's 4th Grade Class

Two teams of three teachers apiece are conducting a walkthrough of Jeffrey Brooks's classroom, which occupies a pie-shaped wedge of an open-concept school that was built to encourage collaboration, innovation, and flexibility. The school has few walls between classrooms, and the conduits for its electrical systems are brightly colored and visible overhead and along its walls. Teachers at the school operate on the theory that it is best to allow students to develop at their own pace in small, challenging learning groups. A staff of caring team teachers using integrated, thematically focused instruction ensures each student's success.

As a black male, Brooks is a member of two demographic groups underrepresented among educators. He is young and athletic, with a close-cropped fade haircut and neatly trimmed mustache. When observers visit his classroom in early January, they find paper snowflakes, flags from around the world, and a three-foot SpongeBob SquarePants toy hanging from the ceiling, making for a physically inviting space. The voices of the surrounding teachers and students seem to float up over the blue and white freestanding room dividers, storage cabinets, and portable blackboards and into Brooks's class. Brooks

himself is seated on a stool next to a multimedia cart on which a video podcast of a lesson on water conservation is playing. When the podcast ends, Brooks reminds the clusters of students seated in groups of three or four at bright maple-topped desks that the podcast provided arguments for saving water and suggested ways to do so.

"You heard at least three ways that you can help save water," says Brooks, before asking for a show of hands from those who recall hearing this information in the podcast. He tells students that today they will be tasked with learning the thinking processes and steps involved in writing an expository paper to explain a favorite pastime to younger children—a task that mirrors what the students will need to do on district and state-level assessments.

After walking to the computer near the front of the room, Brooks opens and projects a Microsoft Word document onto a screen. He types "How to Be a Good Juggler," the date, and the name of the author (SpongeBob SquarePants). As he types, he remarks that it's a new year and asks students whether they had a good winter holiday. Brooks is personally inviting and demonstrates a level of caring that is essential to establishing a positive context for learning. He returns to the lesson by asking the class, "Is that a good beginning?" Several students respond, "Yeah!" Brooks has purposely inserted a few spelling and formatting errors in the document, so he asks the students what SpongeBob SquarePants has gotten wrong. As students raise their hands to volunteer corrections, Brooks approaches them with a microphone. As they speak into the mike, Brooks types their suggested changes into the document. By using questions and recitation, Brooks maintains active student learning and takes advantage of students' preferences for verbal expression.

Brooks focuses students' attention on the task at hand, reminding them to write their names on the pages in their journals and letting them know that they will be creating an outline or a concept web before writing a draft of their papers. He tells students that making an outline is as easy as making a list, and inserts four numbered lines in the document. He then probes to elicit students' ideas about the content to include in the paper.

"Now if I want to be a good juggler, what's the first thing I should write about?" he asks. Moving his hands as if juggling imaginary objects, he repeats: "'How to be a good juggler,'" adding, "We've got some good jugglers in here, right? Xavier?"

"You will need three objects," says Xavier. Repeating Xavier's statement while typing it into the document, Brooks asks students to suggest objects to juggle. With each suggestion—ping pong balls, clubs, and chainsaws—Brooks repeats the terms as he types them.

Next, Brooks asks, "What is the second thing I should write about? What else?" He calls on Lena, who says, "Start with one ball." Brooks repeats her words as he writes them in the document. "Okay," he continues. "What's another step? You need three objects, you start with one ball. Julianna, what else?"

Julianna moves her hands in a crisscross pattern and replies, "Move the ball like this."

Brooks asks, "What's that motion? An X motion?" The class replies in unison: "Yeah!"

Then Brooks asks, "Will a kindergartener, 1st grader, or 2nd grader know what the X motion is?" The class, again in unison, responds with a resounding "No!" Brooks continues: "So if you're going to write about juggling, you're going to have to carefully explain the procedure, right?"

As Brooks types "Use the X motion" into the document, a student named Chris waves his hands and says, "Oh, oh! You have to *practice*!"

"When Mr. C. taught me how to juggle, I practiced and watched a juggling video," says Brooks. "Practice is important, too, right? Learning tricks? Let's write that: 'Practice and learn tricks.' So now I have my outline. You guys will have to do that, too. That's the first thing you'll need, right? Begin now. You are going to start writing your own outline or concept web."

As students move around the room, going to their desks to pull out writing journals, Brooks projects a PowerPoint file onto the screen that lists the directions for the activity. "Remember what we said as we started," he says. "Think about something you like to do or are really good at—playing a musical instrument, for instance. The key idea here is to explain this pastime to someone you don't know and who doesn't know anything about it. Take a look at the directions."

In keeping with best practices in classroom-based assessment, Young prepares his students for success on district and state assessments by regularly providing them with opportunities to practice responding to writing tasks that mirror the format, style, and level of difficulty of those tests. The slide on the screen reads as follows:

Expository Writing

Think of something you like to do or are very good at.

This could be a sport, a craft, or a musical instrument.

Your assignment is to write a paper about this activity for someone who doesn't know anything about it.

Be sure to include procedures on how to perform the activity.

Brooks circulates around the room, stopping at students' tables to look at their work, ascertain progress, ask questions, and offer hints. In doing this, he ensures that all students understand their individual roles in content mastery and task completion steps. To Anna, he advises: "We're not doing a first draft yet. We're just doing our outline." Stopping at Jamil's desk, he asks: "What did you choose: a web or an outline?" Moving to another table, he asks: "Andre, what did you choose? Doing a handstand?"

Having made his way back to the front of the room, Brooks draws the class's attention to the screen and reads the directions aloud again. Highlighting in yellow the words "something you like to do or are very good at" and "for someone who doesn't know anything about it," he notes, "Those words are key."

Circulating among the students again, Brooks talks to Robin and announces to the class, "Robin is going to write about how to play the flute. Beautiful!" He then questions Robin to find out the steps she will describe to her reader. Moving on to Maya, he asks, "So, Maya, what about singing? What's the first step to singing?" As Brooks repeats her response—"Make sure you have a good voice"—Maya adds, "You have to feel emotional about it." Brooks moves closer to the table and says, "'Emotional.' That's a big word. What does that mean?" Maya rests her chin on her hand and responds, "Happy, sad, mad." Brooks repeats her words to the rest of the table and asks Robin to recall her feelings during a recent performance in which she sang for the school. She reports that she felt "half happy and half sad" because of the message of the song. Through oral communications like this one with Maya, Brooks uses continuous, frequent assessments to determine students' levels of skills and knowledge, provide feedback on goals attainment, and create interventions for students who need them. Walking away, Brooks invites Maya to think about whether being an actress requires one to be emotional. He then warns the class that there are two minutes left to complete the activity.

Brooks's students use a variety of modes of representing information and ideas, including graphic organizers such as concept webs and advance organizers such as outlines. One of Brooks's students, who has decided to write about soccer, creates the graphic outline shown in Figure 4.1.

Back at the computer, Brooks announces, "I know some of us are not done, but please put your pencils down. What's up, Nickie? Ready, Javier?" He calls out students' names to recognize and engage them and to promote a positive social context for learning by being personally inviting and caring. "Now, this is my first draft. Can you see, Elena?" Brooks reads aloud as he types, "This is how to be a good juggler." Drawing on his students' preference for group participation and sharing, he asks the class whether this is a good start and whether he has forgotten anything. A student named Marquis advises him to indent his paragraph. Following and repeating Marquis's advice, he again asks the class for any suggestions. This exchange provides the modeling and practice that Brooks believes his students will need prior to their having to demonstrate their understanding during independent practice.

Showing that his students share his ability to develop well-written text and that he shares the power to evaluate the quality of written text with them, Brooks asks, "Did someone have a *better* beginning? Ali? Rosa? Zachariah?" Brooks makes it a point to call on every student regularly. When he calls on Brian, Brian responds with a new opening, to which Brooks expresses delight. He asks the class, "Did you hear what he said? Say it again, Brian." Brian says, "You want to be a great juggler? Follow these steps." Brooks repeats his words and types them into the projected document. By doing this, he ensures that his students share important roles and demonstrate their expertise to their peers. When he asks the students if Brian's suggestion is an improvement on the original, almost all of them raise their hands. Agreeing with them, Brooks concedes, "The first opening was okay, but this one is even better."

Figure 4.1 Sample Graphic Organizer for Paper on Soccer

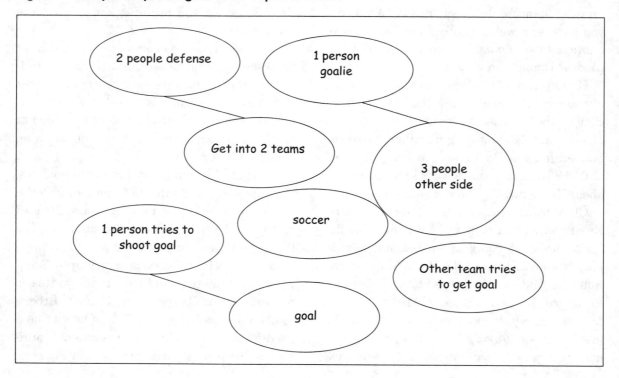

To model the next step, Brooks says, "Remember that you are writing to a 1st or 2nd grader. This little kid doesn't know anything about juggling." He calls on Julius to tell the class how the next sentence should read. Julius suggests that they write, "First, you need three objects." Brooks walks over to a poster on the wall contrasting narrative and expository writing (see Fig. 4.2). Pointing to the column labeled "Expository Writing," he reminds students that they will "need explanation and details." By displaying this poster and having students learn how to distinguish between and write in two different modes, Brooks aligns instruction and curriculum content to the students' authentic knowledge and skills as well as to the assessment methods used in statewide assessments.

Brooks returns to the computer and reads the sentence "First, you need three objects." Promoting a collaborative approach to learning, he asks several students what he needs to do next. Brooks engages his students through reciprocal teaching, in which students gradually assume the role of teacher and help their peers construct meaning. He asks them to consider whether younger students will understand the meaning of the word "object." The students say that younger readers will not understand the word, so several suggest replacing it with "thing." Brooks replaces the word and reads the new sentence aloud: "First you need three things." He asks, "See what we're doing? We're making the words simpler." Brooks then encourages students to add the next sentences that will tell the younger learners how to start juggling their objects. He asks, "Would younger kids be able to juggle all three things at once?" When the students respond with a resounding "No!" he asks, "So what should we tell the 1st and 2nd graders?" Josie offers, "They should *start* with just two things." Brooks asks the rest of the students what they think. Several chime in: "Yeah, start with just *two* things" and "If they start with more, they'll just drop them." Brooks then calls on Caleb, who is waving his hands furiously. Caleb notes that talking

Figure 4.2 Content of Poster Contrasting Narrative and Expository Writing

Narrative Writing . . .	Expository Writing . . .
• Is entertaining	• Is informative
• Could be funny or fantastical	• Is not fictional
• Is descriptive	• Is based on research
• Requires	• Explains things
○ a problem	• Includes details
○ a beginning, middle, and an end	• Describes what things are like (color, shape, size)
○ Interesting characters	• Can be in list form (first, second, third)
○ Capitals, periods, question marks, etc.	• Requires capitals, periods, commas, etc.

about dropping things makes him think that 2nd graders should first learn how to toss one item into the air while holding onto another item. Brooks asks the students if they agree, and most of the class yells out "Yes!" Concurring, Brooks asks Caleb how to write down what he just said before reading Caleb's contribution aloud to the class: "First, you need two things. You can't start juggling both things in the air at the same time, so first toss the one in your right hand into the air. While that one is in the air, toss the item from your left hand to your right hand. With your empty left hand, you can now quickly catch the item that was in the air." Brooks demonstrates with two rubber balls and asks the class to follow his motions with imaginary balls.

Demonstrating how to add more explanation, Brooks adds and reads aloud, "Your thing does not have to be a ball." For the next sentence, which describes what the thing might be, he solicits and writes down the students' suggestions, expressing delight or puzzlement as they yell them out: bowling pins, eggs, clubs, rings, scarves, and so on. Brooks interjects that they will use commas because they are writing a series of items. When Julius and Ali suggest plastic chickens, he asks the class if live chickens are an option, to which they respond "No!" Agreeing that it would be hard to juggle live chickens, Brooks asks the class to suggest fruits; a few call out "apples!" and "watermelons!" Calling for the last suggestions, Brooks asks the class which word needs to be written just before that last object. The students shout out "and" in unison. When he asks for the last item in the list, one student yells, "mini-plungers!" Allowing the last volunteer to slip into the role of teacher, Brooks

asks her what a mini-plunger is. When she is finished describing it, Brooks reports that he has learned something new. After congratulating the students on the list, Brooks asks, "Is that a pretty good paragraph?" the class shouts, "Yeah!"

As the observers leave the classroom, Brooks brings his meaningful and relevant learning activity to a close. He announces with a smile, "It's reading time; we'll continue this activity tomorrow. I am *reading* now."

Walkthrough Wrap-Up

Before convening in the teachers' workroom for a facilitated feedback session, the walkthrough teams gather in the hallway outside Brooks's classroom, taking a few minutes to make checks next to strategies that they observed on their individual feedback forms and to add to the notes they made. Then, the observers share the notes that they wrote at the bottom of their forms, in the section titled "What Teachers/Students Say/Do Related to the Focus Area." Here's what the teachers found:

Teacher 1
Focus: Self-Efficacy
Findings: Teacher 1 recalled that Brooks demonstrated his confidence in the students' ability to complete the assigned writing task, and that he was ebullient in his feedback when he heard that Robin would be writing about how to play the flute. Teacher 1 also noted that Brooks fostered students' responsibility for the writing assignment by repeatedly drawing their attention to the screen and reading the directions aloud. In addition to modeling

and guiding students as they planned their papers, Brooks showed students that they shared his ability to develop and evaluate the quality of written text by asking for their input for the sample paper.

Teacher 2

Focus: Social Interactions

Findings: Teacher 2 noted the overwhelmingly positive social interactions in Brooks's class. He used a short social interlude at the beginning of class to reconnect with students, asking whether they had had a good winter holiday. Brooks also shared personal experiences relevant to the lesson with his students, such as when he discussed how Mr. C. had taught him to juggle.

Teacher 2 found Brooks to be personally inviting, using a humorous tone throughout the lesson, such as when he said, "It's reading time; we'll continue tomorrow. I am *reading* now." He demonstrated the caring that is essential to establishing a positive context for learning, encouraging students to engage in the lesson by calling on them by name and repeating their contributions out loud. Brooks expressed delight with student suggestions that might advance their understanding of the task or ability to evaluate their work.

Teacher 3

Focus: Classroom Management

Findings: Teacher 3 found that although Brooks used appropriate adult language to help students understand task requirements and clarified time limits and other performance expectations, he did not have to discipline any students, who seemed to clearly understand their roles.

Teacher 4

Focus: Assessment

Findings: Teacher 4 noted that many of the teacher-student interactions in Brooks's class were related to classroom-based assessment. In keeping with best practices, Brooks intentionally prepared his students to succeed on district and state assessments by having the writing task mirror the format, style, and level of difficulty of the assessments. Moreover, Brooks aligned instruction and curriculum content to the authentic knowledge and skills used by writers, helping students understand the characteristics of expository writing. Brooks circulated among students, providing continuous feedback on their progress and offering hints, prompts, and questions as interventions for students who needed them. He also helped students develop their ability to self-assess by asking questions such as, "Is that a good beginning?" and encouraging students to edit the sample paper.

Teacher 5

Focus: Cultural Congruence

Findings: Teacher 5 was intrigued by the way Brooks scaffolded student learning by using hand gestures to mimic juggling, and noticed that he continually relied upon students' current understanding of juggling. Brooks also took advantage of students' preferences for verbal expressiveness to help them elaborate on possible juggling items.

Teacher 6

Focus: Procedures for Presenting Processing and Transferring Learning

Findings: Teacher 6 noticed that Brooks spent the bulk of his time helping students to internalize the processes necessary for independently developing a four-paragraph expository paper. By using questions and recitation, Brooks promoted active student learning, and by encouraging the use of graphic organizers, he helped students organize their thinking. Teacher 6 found that Brooks used technology in the form of PowerPoint to provide modeling and guided practice for students. He also began class with a podcast that mirrored the task that students were to perform. Teacher 6 was also impressed with the way Brooks maintained active learning by repeatedly calling for extended, substantive responses, such as when he called on students to suggest objects they might juggle or called upon random students in the class.

5

Curriculum and Instructional Design

In this chapter, we will examine how the PTP educators implemented the following strategies:

Category: Alignment of Goals, Standards, Instruction, and Assessment
Strategies: Teachers . . .
- Develop clear goals and standards.
- Design instruction aligned to curriculum content and authentic assessment methods.
- Align assessments to the content, format, and complexity or level of difficulty of teaching and learning activities.

Category: Careful Instructional Planning
Strategies: Teachers . . .
- Carefully plan and clearly structure day and lesson content.
- Structure lessons to include review of mastered material.
- Use varied systematic strategies for direct reading instruction, such as using encoding principles and maintaining an upbeat climate.

Category: Planning for Student Engagement
Strategies: Teachers . . .
- Carefully plan the day and lessons to include active engagement.
- Design structured classes and daily routines.

- Have and state specific and explicit activity objectives.
- Balance facilitation of student learning with teacher-centered presentations to the whole class.
- Help arouse student curiosity by helping students understand the purpose of learning content.

Category: Personalized Instruction

Strategies: Teachers . . .
- Plan activities to meet the individual developmental needs of diverse students.
- Allow students to share in lesson planning.

Category: Planning for Cooperative Group Instruction

Strategies: Teachers . . .
- Structure environments for cooperative learning and group activities.
- Structure group tasks to ensure that students share important roles and develop expertise.
- Structure group composition to balance familiar and unfamiliar group members.
- Ensure that group goals are attainable.

Aligning Goals, Standards, Instruction, and Assessment

PTP teachers carefully aligned curriculum, instruction, and content to standards and to classroom-based and high-stakes assessments. Many researchers have found that this type of alignment, when coupled with careful instructional planning that takes into account students' development needs, is essential for helping to close the achievement gap between black and white students (Hollins & Spencer, 1990; Irvine & Armento, 2001; Ladson-Billings, 1994; Pasch, Sparks-Langer, Gardner, Starko, & Moody, 1991).

Schoolwide Systems of Articulated and Aligned Curriculum

Students are best served when they work alongside teachers to come up with educational objectives. As PTP middle school principal Alicia Baldwin noted, student achievement "is tied to the articulated standards—making sure that teachers and students know what students need to know and be able to do at each grade." Elementary school principal Patrice Tam mentioned that teachers at her school helped meet the academic, social, and emotional needs of their diverse populations by tracking achievement on standards, assessing all students biannually to find out their individual needs in content areas using such tools as the Individual Reading Inventory (IRI), and conducting collaborative grade-level meetings to analyze student work.

Elementary school principal Darrell Conway emphasized the importance of addressing the specific multiple intelligences most common to black students— musical, kinesthetic, and interpersonal—when planning instruction. "The problem is not that the children can't learn," he said, "but that teachers can't teach in a variety of ways." Conway's school featured a full inclusion model with heterogeneous classrooms and teachers willing to teach to all of the multiple intelligences. Diana Granger, a 4th grade teacher at Conway's school, said that staff members there worked together to create written standards that supported cooperative learning, critical thinking, multiple intelligences, and the use of technology. The criteria for each of the school's standards were divided into three developmental levels—one each for high, medium, and low development.

Individual Approaches Driven by Schoolwide Curriculum and Philosophies

"Although there are lots of standards and multiple ways to engage my students, the perspective from which I approach everything I do is, 'What can I do? What do I find valuable that I can use to keep students engaged?'" said middle school teacher David Maslin. "I pick through standards to find an entry point, but instruction is always based on what will work to engage students. Next, I find out what kids are missing out on and add that to their experience. What I find is that you have to offer *more* than the specified state or district grade-level curriculum."

Elementary school principal Tate Fischer said 4th grade teacher Christie Wyatt was knowledgeable about and "focused totally on and teaching to standards. She front-loads instruction by continually diagnosing student needs." Regardless of the varying needs of students, PTP educators had faith in their abilities. Middle school teacher Jessica Wakefield asserted that she made clear her belief in her students' capacity to meet standards: "I tell

them that I see them all as individuals. I'm going to help them achieve. I make it clear to them that although they have different backgrounds, the expectations are the same."

Careful Instructional Planning

Middle school teacher Charles Ackerman began every school year by developing a curriculum plan and a schedule for how he and students would progress toward meeting desired learning standards. His lessons tended to be conceptually connected and interdisciplinary, focusing on multicultural themes in music and mathematics. He found that planning lessons carefully helped him to scaffold his students' development, meet students' motivational needs, provide variety, and create activities that mirrored those on high-stakes tests.

Flexibility was the key to Jessica Wakefield's ability to plan lessons that helped students master content standards. Her principal, Kim Hanh Nguyen, credited Wakefield's success to her content knowledge, intuition, ability to learn from experience, and her organization skills. In addition, Wakefield continuously assessed her students to monitor their progress and applied new instructional strategies when those that she used failed to work.

Using Varied Systematic Strategies for Direct Reading Instruction

Direct reading instruction among PTP educators was heavily informed by training that the educators received from the National

Urban Alliance (NUA) as part of a multiyear, districtwide literacy initiative. The training helped educators to learn factors that influenced the social, emotional, physical, and academic development of black students; to consider the various meanings that students might draw from text depending on their demographic backgrounds; and to integrate varied instructional strategies in their lesson planning.

Elementary school principal Joanne Stewart noted that, when planning literacy instruction, 3rd grade teacher Mark Goldberg "examined the strategies presented in the literacy initiative quite closely before taking responsibility for incorporating specific techniques that he believed would work for kids." In addition to using direct instruction, Stewart said, Goldberg incorporated such culturally relevant accelerated learning techniques as recitation and call and response.

Middle school principal Alicia Baldwin noted that teachers Marian Katz and Carla Storey both used the NUA literacy strategies to help students practice, process, and transfer information using multiple methods that supported students' individual needs. For instance, Baldwin reported observing Katz's students engaged in minilessons on reading and writing skills at specially designed stations. The rigor and content of these lessons varied over the years as Katz made adjustments in response to students' needs, abilities, and learning styles.

In Storey's classroom, Baldwin observed the frequent use of graphic organizers. Storey said that she presented carefully planned lessons to strengthen students' skills and review content related to standards, "making clear connections between reading and writing and using specific warm-ups such as writing in science notebooks." To help arouse students' curiosity about the purpose and practical intent of her lessons, Storey engaged them in discussions about "what we will learn in the next lesson and why, and whether or not our daily objectives have been met."

Planning for Student Engagement and Personalized Instruction

Third grade teacher Kimberly Lazarides found activities that "keep kids active" to be especially effective with her black students. "They don't want to always just sit and listen during a lecture," she said, "so I make an effort to engage them in projects." According to elementary school principal Rosalie de la Cruz, 4th grade teacher Mark Donnelly "provided practical applications where kids are up, out, and doing things." Donnelly incorporated his students' preferences for collaboration on kinesthetic learning activities in his planning for science instruction. "He'll present students with information from the National Science Foundation using wood products," said de la Cruz. "His kids are working in cooperative problem-solving groups to collaboratively conduct inquiry-based investigations." De la Cruz noted that Donnelly actively taught students how to conduct each aspect of a given investigation "by asking, 'Why is that?' 'Why did those events occur?' 'How were problems solved?' and 'What do you think?' to arrive at solutions. He plans activities with a problem-solving format and uses a constructivist approach with the kids' knowledge as the basis for inquiry." Donnelly allowed students to use both oral and written communication in his class and asked students to explain the answers to the questions explored during their investigations and experiments in their journal-writing exercises.

The Power of Making Objectives Explicit and Arousing Students' Curiosity

PTP educators strengthened their students' motivation to achieve by actively planning ways to arouse their students' curiosity about the purpose behind each day's learning activities. "Kids are more vested when they realize that there is a relevant reason to do what they're asked to do," said Alicia Baldwin. One of the teachers at Baldwin's school, Mick Denby, posted a purpose statement on the board that read as follows: *We are going to work on these strategies because this will make it quicker and easier for you to do your math.* Baldwin noted that the statement "got the kids to buy in to the fact that they'll be able to do complex operations in a quicker, more efficient manner. Kids want to know what's in it for them. After Mick made his lessons relevant for all the kids, I saw that they started to work a little harder."

Clarifying the purpose of lessons is especially important for young black male students. "They have to see *what* they need to do and know *why* they are doing a lesson—what's in it for them," said Baldwin. "Teachers need to know that black boys who are less connected to the culture of school are not going to do classroom work just for their own good. They need to know *why* they need to do it, why they need to learn it, or *they're not going to do it.*"

Denby said that he "grounded math instruction as much as possible in real-world examples and applications that kids will encounter at their levels and in their lives." For example, he valued the school's selection of the Connected Math Program because of its reliance upon a "contextual, experiential-based approach to mathematics. I fell in love with the lesson format that has students look at a situation that shows them a reason for needing the math. For example, when we studied rates or percentages, I talked about record stores and what the kids encounter when making purchases there."

Balancing Facilitation of Student Learning with Teacher-centered Presentations to the Whole Class

Third grade teacher Glen Roberts considered his position as a guide for student-centered interactions to be an expression of his teaching philosophy. "He lets them wonder on their own with his guidance," said his principal, Mai Pham. "He lets them make decisions and solve problems based on data they've gathered," thus developing individual expertise. Roberts recalled spending a significant amount of class time helping students understand their individual roles in making choices and meeting behavioral and academic expectations.

Personalizing Instruction and Planning Activities to Meet the Individual Developmental Needs of Diverse Students

Mark Donnelly used continuous assessment to try to figure out what kind of learners his students were. "I watch them to see who's listening, who's visual, who's fidgeting—those are likely kinesthetic learners," he said. "I've noticed that large numbers of kinesthetic learners—mostly boys—show their style preferences by doing things like fiddling with the goodies in their desks." Donnelly went so far as to schedule conferences with his students "to allow them to talk about their learning styles" and allow him to "tell them how they can use their preferred styles to their advantage."

After Donnelly had a chance to observe his students and plan some instructional activities, he made it clear to students that they needed to choose how to be engaged in class. For example, he said, "I don't mind if they stand or need to sit on the floor." At the same time, he decided when the workload necessitated placing students in heterogeneous groups to complete problem-solving tasks collaboratively.

Equitable Access through Full Inclusion

At Diana Granger's school, providing equitable access to learning opportunities for all students meant the institution of a full-inclusion model. She and her team partner planned activities to meet the needs of a diverse range of students, including "two behaviorally disturbed kids who are in the classroom all day, some children who are labeled emotionally disturbed, a little boy who is mentally retarded, and the regular education students." Granger found that the presence of an articulated curriculum, differentiated learning groups, and learning centers was instrumental to reducing the number of behavior problems at the school. "When we ensure that all the differentiated lessons are present and the kids are engaged, the behavior problems become fewer and fewer," she said.

Planning for Cooperative Group Instruction

Principal Alicia Baldwin noted that teachers at her school created strong, cohesive environments through affirmations, humor, and support, and focused on ensuring that "students could work together to assist each other in learning." She also found that her teachers valued social interactions so highly that "they treated learning about social interactions like an academic pursuit."

Teachers Diana Granger and Gillian Novak said that they made an effort to teach students how to build relationships with each other so that students could learn to trust each other as learning partners. As principal Patrice Tam noted, trusting partnerships among students support the beliefs that everyone is capable of making contributions to group learning efforts, that "each child has gifts," and that teachers and students are in classrooms to "help each other."

Because of his belief that student learning should be grounded in social relationships, Ryan Toth seated his students in groups mixed by disposition, compatibility, race, gender, and ability. His seating arrangement served two major purposes. First, it helped his students "to be happy and get along with each other." Second, it helped them to develop a collaborative approach to learning in which they sought and provided assistance to each other before going to him. To increase the likelihood that his students could assist each other, Toth placed "higher achieving students with kids who have some problems in areas so that whenever they were working, they could look to the person next to them for help."

Toth found cooperative group work to be especially effective with black students. "They really liked the interactions with other students, discussing the work before moving on to complete the steps in a task," he said. "They really liked the discussion aspect, and I felt oftentimes that my job as a teacher was just to guide them."

For middle school teacher Lisa Forsythe, the beginning of the school year was a time to actively teach her students the features of the physical environment that needed to be in place to support cooperative group work. Forsythe purposefully taught lessons on expectations, procedures, and structures of her classroom (e.g., how to move students' desks into groups of two and four, and then how to put them back out into rows).

Elementary school principal Owen Callahan frequently saw Jeffrey Brooks's students working together in cooperative groups to solve problems, answer questions, and develop content-area knowledge. "I like having students do a lot of group work because they like interacting with each other," said Brooks. He preferred grounding a lesson's format in students' preference for group cohesion and collaboration to simply lecturing to students. "Group work can take care of some management issues," he said. "For instance, if you have one student out of four who is goofing around, the other three will say, 'Hey, let's get to work.'"

Ensuring that Group Members Share Important Roles

Ryan Toth said that he had his students work in cooperative groups as often as possible because he valued the understandings that they could construct in such arrangements. To ensure success and promote student motivation around group tasks, he said that he often began by "presenting a global idea or essential question to the class. To recall prior knowledge and to see what they know, I then like to do a lot of brainstorming." Finally, he would pose a meaningful and engaging question to the class and have students work in groups to arrive at an answer.

Toth noted that, in some cases, his "high-achieving math kids tended to be the ones who would get into a bit of trouble for acting out. It might be that they're energetic, or it's just their style to be very active." Toth used this knowledge to benefit the group. "What I do is I put them to work," he said. "And I've basically taught these kids how to work with others and how to give them clues without giving them the answer. I've made them the first people to go to in their groups. The other students come over, sit, and problem solve with them. And they're fantastic." These student experts share important tasks and develop personal expertise while scaffolding student learning for their peers.

Fourth grade teacher Chloe Gifford shared an example of a task in which students assisted each other in learning one of the culturally relevant literacy strategies she'd learned from the NUA trainings. "We'd been studying the Lewis and Clark expeditions for a week or two," she said. "Students were using a thinking map to create a taxonomy that would help to scaffold their new learning to prior knowledge. First, I had kids individually come up with all the words they could recall related to Lewis and Clark. Quietly, they'd come up with words that start with each letter in the taxonomy. Then, we would do *pollination*—a collaborative group learning strategy in which students assist each other by walking around the room, quietly look at other kids' papers, and, like bees picking up pollen from flowers, picking up words. Then the kids would go back to their seats and add the words that they picked up or that they might have forgotten to their papers. The main purpose is accomplished—students recall and share important information about the topic."

Allowing students to assist each other was just one way that teachers ensured that learning tasks were doable and objectives were attainable. Sixth grade teacher Danielle Kaplan liked to set clear, incremental goals for completing tasks, with multiple interim deadlines. If, for example, students were researching and writing term papers for which they were to make oral presentations to the class, Kaplan would make a PowerPoint presentation outlining the steps; post the presentation on her Web page; provide rubrics showing what students were to do before, during, and after the research; and contrast examples of poor and exemplary work. This approach had the benefits of ensuring that students understood their individual and group roles in task completion; making the expectations accessible to most students at all times, via the Web page; allowing students to share important roles in their own learning and that of their peers; and incorporating some students' preferences for verbal expressiveness in sharing their final products.

Principal Kim Hanh Nguyen saw teacher David Maslin sharing responsibility for teaching with students and students providing assistance to each other as they learned. Nguyen noted that reciprocal teaching of this sort helped students to get organized for group work, find and acquire relevant materials, and assume specific roles that helped their peers to gain and process information. Maslin regularly reminded students that learning would be rigorous and challenging, that they would be responsible for monitoring their individual and group efforts toward achieving learning goals.

6

Classroom-Based Assessment

In this chapter, we will examine how the PTP educators implemented the following strategies:

Teachers . . .
- Align instruction and curriculum content to authentic assessment methods.
- Align assessments to the content, format, and complexity or level of difficulty of teaching and learning activities.
- Use frequent continuous assessments to determine skills and knowledge, provide feedback on goals attainment, and create interventions.
- Augment standardized tests with a variety of assessment strategies appropriate to diverse learners, including observations, oral examinations, and performances.
- Make decisions using multiple samples of students' best efforts toward meeting standards, consistently scored against public criteria.
- Teach students how to self-assess and monitor development of skills, knowledge, and dispositions.
- Use culturally sensitive, fair, and unbiased assessments of cognitive and social skills.
- Match assessment to students' language and home culture.

• Ensure that language abilities and special needs do not interfere with demonstration of competence by providing coaching, accommodations, and translation support as needed.
• Vary content, time, and format of assessment sessions in response to students' energy levels and engagement patterns.

PTP educators, like educators throughout the United States, are acutely aware that their competence and the efficacy of their schools are evaluated against requirements of the No Child Left Behind (NCLB) Act. Further, Asa Hilliard (2004) notes that over the past few decades educators have become more aware of ways to more equitably assess disadvantaged students, including a deeper understanding of the various purposes of assessment and "cognitive change" approaches to teaching and learning.

Attention to alignment of valid, authentic assessments to curriculum content and instructional methods is one of the key factors to which PTP teachers attribute increases in black students' achievement. Such alignment necessitates specifying the curriculum content and narrowing the number of specific goals that students are to meet. PTP teachers succeeded in promoting high achievement among their students in part by matching assessment to instruction—that is, testing the way they taught. For example, 3rd grade teacher Mark Goldberg reported "appraising the developmental level of each child" relative to instructional goals and creating "small chunks of instructional time directed toward achieving specific objectives or skills."

PTP teachers also examined the extent to which what and how they taught reflected the broadest possible understanding of the learning targets within the disciplines. For example, students in Mark Donnelly's 4th grade mathematics/social studies class were not simply taught how to draw and measure lines, but also how to use those skills to create perspective drawings and scale models of an 18th-century New England town that they were studying. What Donnelly taught and tested was consistent with his personal philosophy of making teaching and learning engaging, his desired learning outcomes, and the needs of his students.

Elementary school principal Patrice Tam noted that her entire staff regularly used "WASL-like" tasks that mirrored state assessment standards and formats to prepare students for high-stakes tests. The scaffolding teachers provided to align classroom-based and district or state assessments took many forms, including modeling, demonstrations, and practice with tasks of increasing difficulty. Tam noted that 4th grade teacher Chloe Gifford began doing explicit "WASL prep in her classroom at the end of January." Gifford's students, like others throughout the school, had been assigned to ability-based reading groups with different teachers from late September on; for the WASL prep, they were reunited with their home teachers. Gifford insisted that her students' weekly homework packets contain engaging problems aligned to the complexity and cognitive demand of the WASL. PTP middle school teacher Susan Lansing also noted that she had students prep for WASL "throughout the year, but with a concentration about eight weeks prior to test" by having them write and score short- and extended-response items similar to those on the WASL.

As recommended by NCLB, PTP teachers' assessments reflected the full range of difficulty, depth, meaning, and rigor represented in the standards. Several PTP educators pointed to their focus on providing explicit instruction on the rigorous vocabulary required in assessments to prevent students' language deficiencies from interfering with their demonstration of competence. Marshall Waters, principal of a K–8 school with a 90 percent black student population, noted that analysis of missed test items at the elementary and middle school levels made it "really evident that our kids don't have the vocabulary development to answer questions. We have found that students' failure on many tasks was *not* due to not knowing how to perform tasks." He stressed that vocabulary-building activities at his school "addressed the deficiencies our black students have in language and vocabulary."

Hilliard (2004), citing Feurstein (1979) and Lidz (2000), notes that "instructionally valid beneficial testing and assessment approaches [such as explicit instruction in vocabulary development] have been available for more than half a century." These approaches, "rooted in the cognitive psychology of Binet and Piaget, [assume] malleable intelligence, and emphasize the [value] of diagnostic cognitive assessment and remedial teaching or mediation." In keeping with these understandings and NCLB guidance, PTP educators created and used different forms of high-quality assessment—pre-assessment, formative assessment, and summative assessment.

Pre-Assessment

Elementary school principal Erdie Baptiste saw 3rd grade teacher Kimberly Lazarides take advantage of pre-assessment to create individual profiles for learners from diverse cultural and academic backgrounds that included data on students' content-area knowledge and learning styles preferences. Baptiste noted that Lazarides's multi-strategy approach included developing a "journey plan for groups of two to six students" based on similar needs in areas such as literacy development. Although Lazarides partnered students with a teacher assistant or tutor to promote collaborative learning assistance, she "didn't rely on second-hand reports, but personally and closely monitored their progress," Baptiste said. Lazarides made her pre-assessment transparent to Baptiste by "regularly reporting progress on individual students" about whom they shared concerns.

Fourth grade teacher Christie Wyatt also used pre-assessment to develop comprehensive views of students' backgrounds by talking to students individually, noticing what they said about their homes, and using the info to augment standardized test data in their school folders. "Luckily, by 4th grade, students are more self-aware, know themselves, and can confirm or refute teachers' beliefs about them," said Wyatt. Pre-assessment yielded important information that Wyatt integrated into learning activities to connect content to students and their families.

Wyatt also believed that it was her job to let students and parents know of her high academic and personal expectations. She reported that she "quickly established a rapport with students' parents" and shared pre-assessment results, enlisting their support "as partners to bring students up to where they should be." Then, during the course of the year, Wyatt used formative assessments to determine what and how much students had learned, refine next steps in instruction to reach learning standards, and provide detailed feedback on progress to students and parents. "I can tell them to their faces what I've found and what they are good at and not so good at," she said, recalling one mother who agreed to receive frequent reports "if she could give me feedback as well."

Third grade teacher Ryan Toth did not review his students' school folders immediately upon starting the year. "I don't look at any reports from previous teachers until after conducting beginning-of-the-year assessments," he said, "because I really want to get the information myself." In addition to spending the first few months of school assessing students' social interactions, Toth completed an interest survey of all students during the first month. To get an overall view of their academic capabilities, he said, "I spend quite a bit of time those first five weeks really trying to gauge each kid's reading, writing, and mathematics skills" using a variety of written tests.

Fourth grade teacher Mark Donnelly actively searched through students' files at the beginning of the year, looking for clues to help him form hypotheses about the students' capabilities. He recalled two black female students who had been in his class two years prior and whose file data contradicted his recollection of their capabilities. When first assigned these students, he "noticed that they exhibited real strong personalities, but

wouldn't do a thing I said. I took a look at their files and found that their grades were low." Aware of the tendency among black students to mask their abilities so as not to "act white," Donnelly noted that "with some kids, I try to figure out if they are covering up abilities. Over time, these girls proved that they were very bright, always raising their hands in class." He believed in what these girls could do: when it was time for them to move up to the next grade, he said, he had them tested for an Advanced Placement class.

Designing Assessments

PTP educators are well aware that a poorly designed assessment—one inconsistent with "relevant, nationally recognized professional and technical standards," as prescribed by NCLB—cannot adequately address the needs of students. Haycock (2008) found that one of the distinguishing features of high performing schools in low-socioeconomic-status districts throughout the United States was the presence of assessments that represented the content, format, and difficulty level of high-stakes tests.

Cultural Responsiveness

PTP teachers modified or adopted well-written feasible assessments to develop a repertoire of tests, allowing them to vary the methods they used to meet students' needs in culturally sensitive ways. For example, middle school teacher Carla Storey selected assessments that fit her students' modal interaction patterns and communication styles. "Black people are storytelling people," said Storey, who is black herself. "We are animated; when we tell stories, we talk with our hands. And students love telling stories. I might have a student who won't write anything, but knows all the answers. However, he likes telling stories—he journals with his mouth instead of his pen. I can assess him orally. When I see his *D* from a previous class, I consider what he's capable of doing, not just the grade." To help her students commit oral stories to text, Storey had them make short written notes. "We make it stick with Post-it notes," she said.

Storey's colleague, Gillian Novak, accommodated students' varied presentation styles by providing oral and written assessment options. For instance, 8th graders who worked in groups to make and describe models showing features of the geographic regions of Washington State "got to stand up, show these products, and showcase their learning verbally." Middle school teacher Lisa Forsythe went as far as taking university courses to perfect her use of scoring rubrics to evaluate students' work portfolios. Her principal, Bridget Lawley, felt that "whenever you use a portfolio, it shows that kids are trusted to self-select evidence of their best work." More important, she thought that it demonstrated that "work is important enough to save, display, and hold onto." Another middle school teacher, Chris Spelman, engaged students in authentic, project-based activities once every quarter. "These projects allow students to develop and demonstrate their learning through multiple entry points," he said. "Rather than saying, 'Here's a test. Write an essay,' I'll give them several different prompts and several ways of using multiple intelligences or the strengths that best suit them to show what they know.

They can then choose how they would like to be assessed on a book."

Observational Assessments

Many PTP teachers relied on continuous observational assessments. Middle school teachers Berkeley McGuire and Jessica Wakefield continually assessed students without their being aware that they were being assessed, using their observations to make adjustments and provide accommodations during instruction. Wakefield was "very good at doing on-your-feet kind of assessments," said her principal, Kim Hanh Nguyen. "She was always monitoring, checking whether the kids were getting it, assessing blank looks, and adjusting instruction."

Fourth grade teacher Jeffrey Brooks continuously augmented standardized tests and gathered data using a variety of authentic classroom-based assessments appropriate to his diverse learners, including observations, oral examinations, and performances. For example, prior to having his students complete written exercises to identify multiples and factors of whole numbers, he would read aloud the meaning and examples of the terms from the textbook while also displaying the relevant text on an overhead projector. Within seconds, he'd have students counting off from 1 to 21 and engaged in a kinesthetic activity in which they stood up as the class counted off multiples of 1 through 10. He would explain to students how to find the next multiple and prompt them to stand at the appropriate time. This participatory activity created an active, enjoyable, memorable learning experience for students and a powerful observational performance assessment for Brooks that helped him to develop future lessons and provide feedback to students on their understanding of the concepts.

Continuous and Frequent Assessment

Middle school teacher David Maslin used continuous and frequent assessment to augment what he learned about students from standardized test data. "I make an initial assessment early on based on my preconceived notions of what kids need," he said. To provide students with equitable access to opportunities to learn, Maslin said, "You have to offer more than the curriculum. After that initial stage, I choose strategies based on continuous assessment. I try out plenty of things that middle school students are interested in, do ongoing spot assessments, and move on."

Bridget Lawley observed a similar strategy in David Lee's classroom. "David rethinks and revises tactics when something doesn't work," she said. "When he's delivered a lesson, he stops with every student and gives encouragement or feedback and asks questions."

Multiple Samples of Students' Best Work

PTP teachers ensured the reliability of their judgments about students' progress toward learning objectives by considering multiple samples of students' best efforts toward meeting standards and scoring them against public criteria. Ensuring sufficient samples of tasks related to valued learning targets contributed to understanding students' progress over time. Moreover, PTP teachers helped students understand the *meaning* of the learning

targets and standards by having them examine the rubrics used to assess their work. For example, Kimberley Lazarides had her students contrast poor and high-quality examples of reading, writing, and mathematics work.

"We're teaching the kids how to take classroom-based assessments and then revise their work to meet standards," said principal Alicia Baldwin. The teachers at her school, she said, helped students understand "what a three looks like, or what an exemplar—a four on a scale of one to four—looks like. I think the things that are going to close the gap are one, having kids know what good work looks like, and two, knowing that they're all expected to perform at that level."

Sixth grade teacher Danielle Kaplan taught her students to use rubrics both before and after they completed their work. "Kids don't always follow directions in tasks," she said, "so I give them the directions twice: in the task directions, and then in the performance criteria in the rubrics." In addition to helping students understand their individual roles in mastering expectations, Kaplan promoted her students' sense of self-efficacy by having them apply evaluative criteria to their individual work as well as to low and exemplary sample responses. "I tell them, '*You* are capable of grading yourselves and seeing how you will do.' Over time, they come to see themselves as scholars and assessors," she said.

Attention to Bias, Fairness, and Sensitivity

Understanding the salience of students' cultural and socioeconomic differences helps teachers immensely in accurately assessing the abilities of diverse student groups. Hilliard (2004) notes that because "testing and assessment are dependent upon communication systems that are tied to language, . . . educators face a particular difficulty in ensuring 'equity' in . . . 'culturally fair' and 'culturally relevant' . . . testing and assessment." He advocates recognizing "the cultural uniqueness" of black American speech, providing variations in how students are allowed to "demonstrate what they know and can do . . . [, and] using cultural material that is familiar to them." Likewise, NCLB urges educators to design and use high-quality assessments that avoid potential bias that could distort assessment results. Analyses of the practices of PTP teachers show that they effectively responded to these recommendations by using well-documented strategies, such as by

- Using culturally sensitive, fair, and unbiased assessments;
- Developing and using assessments that adhere to fairness and sensitivity guidelines;
- Ensuring that language abilities and special needs do not interfere with students' abilities to demonstrate their competence by providing coaching, accommodations, interpretation, and translation support as needed; and
- Providing accommodations for special learning needs, such as varying the content, times, and format of assessment sessions in response to students' energy and engagement patterns.

Often, teachers work in district or regional teams to develop classroom-based assessment that mirrors the format, content, and level of difficulty of high-stakes assessments. Over the past 10 years, I myself have facilitated such teams, which are tasked with removing stereotypes or negative representations of demographic groups; over- or under-representation of groups; or wording that may be confusing, offensive, or unfamiliar to students.

Principal Erdie Baptiste detailed how Kimberly Lazarides worked to ensure that the language abilities and special needs of an African refugee student who spoke only French did not interfere with his ability to demonstrate competencies. Lazarides "saw the potential in the child," Baptiste said, and "enlisted the assistance of district office translators to provide "interpretation and translation support."

When I visited Berkley McGuire's class, I found her helping her class of mostly English-language learners prepare for a classroom-based science assessment. Students worked in small groups to craft oral presentations on their findings in a science investigation. In addition to science content and inquiry skills, communication standards would be assessed. McGuire gave students two opportunities to present their findings: after the first presentation, she provided multiple feedback sessions detailing students' progress, and over the next week, students revised their oral and written reports and presented them to the class after they and McGuire were satisfied with them.

Nearly every PTP school provided similar kinds of scaffolding, accommodations, and supports for assessments. Principal Bridget Lawley recalled that staff at her school encouraged student interest in the WASL by "having a kick-off assembly." To ensure that students didn't become too anxious when test time rolled around, she said, her staff "made sure kids were tested in classrooms with teachers they knew." In addition, because Lawley and her staff knew the benefits of nutrition to student engagement and perseverance on tasks, they "provided them with food and 'WASL Water.'" Staff also accommodated special learning needs by varying the times and formats of assessment sessions. Lawley scheduled testing so that teachers "used the entire testing window and blocked out time to provide extended testing sessions" as students needed them.

Involving Parents as Assessment Partners

Ryan Toth and his co-teacher used multiple techniques to enlist parents' help with assessing student progress, including discussions at Open House, devoting newsletter columns to writing assessment, sending home ideas to help parents to discuss what students are learning, and developing a weekly writing assignment that mirrored both classroom-based and high-stakes assessment tasks. Toth said his students' successes were attributable in large part to collaboration with parents and discussions with them about benchmarks. "We work with parents to help the students," he said, "so parents and teachers can hold the kids accountable at both ends."

Involving Students as Assessment Partners

PTP teachers meaningfully involved students as partners, conferring a high degree of agency

upon them in assessing their own learning. Principal Alicia Baldwin observed that Carla Storey helped "students understand learning objectives through practice with criteria and rubrics," and that providing such opportunities helped students to practice prior to high-stakes tests. Storey herself found that when she "helped them to learn test-taking and self-assessment skills, they are encouraged. They do so well."

Principal Bridget Lawley noted that David Lee's students and parents place a lot of value on his progress reporting techniques, from daily turnaround on homework to a cumulative-score wall chart using student ID numbers that Lee updated daily. In addition, Lee spent an hour a week generating progress reports. Middle school teacher Kevin Friedman found end-of-the-year assessments motivating to students who had worked together in various skills-based groups during the year because "they really can see how far they have come."

Involving Peers as Assessment Partners

Elementary school principal Patrice Tam was enthusiastic about her staff's focus on sharing student work, noting that it helped deepen teachers' understanding of their four-point rubric for measuring achievement of the standards. Tam attributed much of her teachers' success to "awareness of and moving students to progress toward achieving the highest levels of the performance standards."

According to Alicia Baldwin, PTP teachers' commitment to examining student work in study groups was particularly powerful.

Teachers at her school partnered with those from neighboring schools to look at student work as a way to improve both professional practice and student achievement. Her staff was particularly interested in understanding the effect of race on achievement. "We look at student work twice a month, and we've been asking teachers to bring in work of students that is problematic," said Baldwin. "We look at the data on the ethnic and racial backgrounds of kids that aren't making it. Teachers ask why certain kids are not making progress on a skill, then problem solve around it."

"These teachers are active in and really believe in study groups," Baldwin continued. "I think that, by looking at student work and deprivatizing practice, people are only going to get better. How do we know how a 4 on a language arts rubric at our school compares to 4 at neighboring schools? That's the type of question we're asking in the study groups." Baldwin saw peer collaboration on examining student assessments as a way of unifying the understanding and diffusion of common performance standards to change instruction and student achievement schoolwide.

7

Cultural Competence

In this chapter, we will examine how the PTP educators implemented the following strategies:

Category: Cultural Understanding and Awareness
Strategies: Teachers . . .
• Understand how race, ethnicity, language, socioeconomic status, gender, history, residential status, and cultural experience influence behavior, performance, and climate.
• Demonstrate knowledge of the modal beliefs, personalities, and interaction, communication, and linguistic styles of varied cultural groups.
• Understand cultural variations and nuances of communication related to verbal and nonverbal cues such as gestures, timing, walking, eye glances, dress, and presentation style.
• Demonstrate knowledge of the diversity of cultural, ethnic, linguistic, and gender groups in the classroom.
• Demonstrate knowledge of students' backgrounds.
• Understand the effect of cultural experience on how students construct knowledge.
• Understand the effect of racism on students.
• Understand aspects of their own culture that facilitate or hinder communication with their own and other cultural groups.

Category: Sensitivity to and Valuing of Cultural Difference

Strategies: Teachers . . .

• Communicate validation and acceptance of cultural and gender differences to students.

• Show genuine respect for cultural pride and diversity.

• Foster students' ability to function in their culture of origin.

Category: Information in Curriculum on Cultural Differences

Strategies: Teachers . . .

• Use curriculum materials that describe historical, social, and political events from a wide range of racial, ethnic, cultural, and language perspectives.

• Investigate topics related to ethnicity, gender, and exceptionality from a wide range of racial, ethnic, cultural, and language perspectives.

• Help each student understand his or her personal perspective, or "self," as one of many cultural perspectives.

• Provide curriculum materials on social, economic, and political issues related to ethnicity, gender, and exceptionality.

• Help students understand how personal and cultural experiences influence how they and others construct knowledge.

• Provide factual information to refute misconceptions and prejudices about ethnic group members.

• Understand and use information about students' families, cultures, and communities to connect to learning activities.

• Encourage mutual sharing of personal and expressive stories related to content.

Category: Cultural Critique and Activism

Strategies: Teachers . . .

• Help students understand, critique, and change social structures and practices that produce inequities.

• Provide opportunities for students to critique concepts learned, their origins, and their authors' economic, political, and social perspectives and motivations.

• Are involved in political struggles aimed at achieving a more just and humane society.

• Urge collective action grounded in cultural understanding, experiences, and ways of knowing the world.

• Help students learn how to change elements of society held up to critique.

• Provide students with experiences making decisions and taking action about real-world problems.

Cultural Understanding and Awareness

Ladson-Billings's research with successful teachers of black students indicates that the following three constructs form the basis of culturally relevant pedagogy: academic achievement, cultural competence, and cultural and sociopolitical critique and activism (1994, 1995). As discussed in Chapter 1, academic achievement concerns teachers' expectations that students will engage and do well in school through challenging, exciting, and reciprocal learning. Cultural competence, according to Ladson-Billings, concerns "the ability to function effectively in one's culture of origin" (1995, p. 465) and to use one's culture to relate to others'. The third construct, cultural and sociopolitical critique and activism, concerns teachers' understandings of the negative effects of racism on black students' ability to perform well in school and to teachers' roles in helping students understand the part that social structures play in replicating inequities.

Numerous researchers affirm that cultural competence is essential to structuring optimal social and academic interactions, establishing cultural congruence between home and school, and enhancing students' cognitive, social, and psychological development (Hollins & Spencer, 1990; Irvine & Armento, 2001; Pasch, Sparks-Langer, Gardner, Starko, & Moody, 1991). This chapter will explore how PTP educators grounded their pedagogical practices in cultural competence.

Celebrating Diversity in the Classroom

Delpit (2000) affirms the earlier findings of Knapp and Turnbull (1991) that culturally competent teachers know, respect, teach about, and help students feel anchored in their individual culture, history, and language; certainly, this was the case among PTP educators. Fourth grade teacher Jeffrey Brooks indicated that, at his school, "We celebrate all cultures by observing ethnic and cultural holidays such as Black History Month, and help kids learn about cultures in the Vietnamese and Spanish classes that they attend." Marshall Waters, principal of an Afrocentric K–8 school, believed that his teachers promoted cultural identification in every class. "Here, each teacher identifies a country in Africa to focus on," he said.

"Our students learn facts about the country, its culture and social norms, how kids play there, how they live, and how their lives are similar to those of our scholars. . . . In every classroom, student identity is on the walls. In addition to displays related to Africa, every classroom features information about and pennants of a different historically black college or university." Waters found that these displays helped "with relationship building and connection among students" and encouraged students to consider "what they want to become."

Third grade teacher Mark Goldberg spoke for many PTP educators when he asserted that he "prized each individual's culture and ethnic background. I try to ensure that each child knows the value of every other child. The kids learn how special each one of us is, and they begin to recognize the cultural part of a person as being important. We never lose sight of who we are as members of an ethnic group. And we as educators definitely never let the kids forget where we as humans come from on the face of the planet: Africa." Goldberg proposed that such genuine respect for cultural diversity allowed "no students to feel that they are less or more than anybody else" and promoted students' treating each other equally well. "I think it is so important to be treated as who we are as individuals," he said, "so we can move forward based on individual skills and really focus on instruction."

Elementary school principal Tate Fischer observed that 4th grade teacher Christie Wyatt projected "a consciousness of culture" in her classroom. Like other PTP teachers, Wyatt was aware that her perspective was that of a white person. Fischer said that this awareness drove Wyatt to be "curious about and communicate effectively with students and parents of all cultural and ethnic groups." Fischer also noted the importance of understanding the "unique styles within learning styles" of black students while also taking care not to stereotype students.

Teacher Knowledge of Students' Backgrounds

PTP educators actively learned about their students' backgrounds to build relationships and foster learning and achievement. To middle school principal Alicia Baldwin, this meant understanding the combinations of economic and cultural factors that affected her students. "For some of my black kids, who are my poorest, it's not that they can't learn or that their learning styles hinder them," she said. "Their performance is really not so much due to their race, but to their socioeconomic status and the opportunities they've been afforded. I have other groups who are certainly in that same position: the Cambodian and Laotian kids in particular. Because my black kids are in the same boat, I think that what improves achievement is teaching them the same background knowledge that their more advantaged counterparts have. We kind of level the playing field."

In discussing teacher Berkeley McGuire, Baldwin again noted the importance of building relationships. "I think that is the single most important piece with any child, the relationship piece," she said. "What makes the PTP teachers stand out is that they know their kids. I can go into a classroom and

Berkeley can tell me three or four personal things about each child." Elementary principal Pham concurs: "Our building is small. Teachers know the kids and their families." Baldwin and McGuire agreed that knowing something about each student's culture was a priority. "I notice traits such as physical appearance, or the attention girls pay to their hair," McGuire said, as well as ethnic and cultural norms of dress and social interaction, "such as with our Muslim students. I work at being genuine, commenting and noticing when a student wants to be noticed. I connect with families on the phone when I call to tell them about homework. I can then use information I learn about students' families to connect to learning outcomes."

PTP educators integrated information about students' backgrounds into instruction in a variety of ways. Middle school principal Alex La Chuisa saw teacher Angela Chaffee draw on students' experiences to help their understanding with math problems. Elementary school principal Owen Callahan noted that 4th grade teacher Jeffrey Brooks "weaved in students' experiences" and incorporated information about their family backgrounds that he garnered from annual student surveys into his classroom. When teachers created the opportunities, they found that students were eager to share information about themselves that could be used to enhance their learning. Middle school teacher Moira Reynolds recalled that when she had students "write about topics in daily journals in U.S. History, they offered insightful connections of the content to their lives. It's a really great way for me to find out what's going on in their lives. It's amazing what they'll write."

Sensitivity to and Valuing of Cultural Differences

Culturally responsive teachers understand the unique qualities of black students' experiences as members of ethnic and cultural groups. As middle school teacher Charles Ackerman put it, while "the human mind learns essentially the same way no matter what, I understand how race, language, or culture might help or interfere with learning." Such understanding is particularly important for white teachers of black students. Christie Wyatt, who is white, reflected on her efforts to dispel negative expectations that her black students might have of her, noting that she benefited from "a lot of coursework in sociology, studying ethnic groups," growing up in multicultural Chicago, and relationships with black people in her family (her brother-in-law and her cousin's husband are black). "I've rubbed elbows with blacks and whites and know something about how they will respond," she said. "Growing up in Chicago, people were very straightforward, so I feel free to ask kids certain things. Kids look at me and think, 'She understands me.'"

One of the most powerful characteristics of effective and culturally responsive teachers is an awareness of their own cultural styles and student biases and how those affect student achievement. PTP educators purposefully and thoughtfully confronted the cultural disparity to which many observers attribute achievement gaps. "With me being a white teacher, a lot of kids come in the room thinking I'm going to treat them differently," said middle school teacher Adrianne Driscoll. Though she said positive and personal relations were important with all students, she observed that "it's a little more important with black students, because they are used to people treating them badly." Middle school teacher Michael Wagner noted that he reflects "all the time on what role I have as a white male teaching minority students. Just who I am—how do they interpret that? And what can I do to not be a roadblock in their learning?"

""I grew up in Montana, where we had one black kid in my school," said 3rd grade teacher Glen Roberts. "In high school, same thing. I find that the more I teach, if I'm honest, the less my biases or prejudices come out, whether they're overt or subconscious. For instance, I see now that my black kids are some of the most exceptional students; before, I would have been surprised by their abilities, or I would have been overly conscious of differences. The more you know people, the more you come to understand the idea that prejudice is based on ignorance. And now that I am immersed in different cultures, I've grown a lot."

Charles Ackerman recalled growing up in Washington's Olympic Peninsula, where the two main ethnic groups were white and Indian. "There were only a handful of black kids in my school, and there were not too many racial incidents between blacks and whites. However, there certainly were racial problems between Indians and whites. I was fortunate because my parents looked down upon racial slurs or treating anybody differently than anybody else. So when I got to Seattle, I was really acclimated. When I began teaching, I really tried to be careful not to say or do the wrong thing to turn people off. As a teacher, it's hard sometimes; you're not even aware, half the time, that you are saying things that are negative to other people because you have these built-in cultural ideas that you learned from your experiences as a child. And while you don't want to necessarily do anything to offend, it's easy enough to do."

Berkeley McGuire agreed. "I'm aware of offensive verbal traits and body language I may present that can be interpreted as offensive and that can hinder interactions. I know that if I'm not inviting in my voice and gestures, or if I'm mean and not firm, it will turn kids off. Students know when I'm firm, fair, and consistent, and they appreciate it. They would notice it if I was not. And because I am, they own up to their choices in our relationship."

Developing Self-Awareness through Professional Learning

PTP educators demonstrated persistence in improving their practice; 26 of the 29 teachers I studied reported engaging in professional development to enhance their sense of cultural competence. Fourth grade teacher Chloe Gifford appreciated the effect of professional learning on her relationships with students and parents. Like many of the other PTP teachers, Gifford was especially affected by her participation in Glen Singleton and Pacific Learning Group's "Courageous Conversations about Race" program, which helped educators examine the effect of race, socioeconomic status, and language on school climate and student behavior and performance. Principal Shannon Weller noted that, during trainings, Singleton challenged educators to imagine their students asking

them, "Look into my eyes. Do you know me?" and to consider the question, "Who are your students' heroes?" Weller argued that the program moved teachers to transcend their typical ways of interacting "to get to the issues important to kids" and to develop caring, positive, and personal student relations.

"I used to say that I was color-blind, but now I know that I'm not," said Gifford. "After the Courageous Conversations program, I understand that there are aspects of my culture that hinder or help communications with parents and kids. And although I'm white, I didn't have the problem of parents saying that students weren't being treated equitably or that I was treating anybody differently. I have great relationships and meaningful collaboration with my parents. I get on the phone right away to parents of kids who are disrespectful. I don't have much problem with that, and parents are very supportive."

Understanding Cultural Styles

PTP educators understood that modal styles and traits vary significantly even within cultural groups. Nonetheless, Carla Storey was convinced that being black herself gave her an advantage with her black students. She noted that she helped her students to see themselves through the lens of their cultural traits. "Black kids are outspoken," she said. "They're verbal; they like stories, anecdotes, and sharing personal experiences. I make those associations with them."

Jeffrey Brooks cautioned that understanding and responding to the modal styles and traits of black students is more complex than espousing generalizations about their ethnic group. "As a black male myself, I don't think my background made a difference in student performance," he said. "There are other schools that have black teachers, and they're not doing so well." He did, however, agree with Storey's comments about linguistic styles: "I do find that black students have a need to express themselves more," he said. Brooks's requirements for order in his classroom are tempered with respect and understanding of his students' traits and backgrounds. "Whereas another teacher might send a certain student to the office because he views that kid's loud talking as a sign of disrespect, I see it's just the way the kid is expressing himself," he said. "If I think about the black kids in my class now, I mean, they're a little loud. But to me, that's just them being themselves. And I could see how another teacher would say, 'Oh, that's being disrespectful.' Personally, I don't let any of the kids get out of hand, but I can see how different teachers interpret their behavior differently."

When considering which instructional strategies were most effective with his black students, 4th grade teacher Mark Donnelly pointed out how diverse those students were. "There's a real mix of kids in my class," he said. "Some are quiet, and some jump around the room. Some can't sit in their chairs." To address this diversity, Donnelly used a variety of strategies while teaching his students to modulate their energy and behavior. He recalled "one boy who was constantly jumping around. He would get quiet, stop jumping around, and get to work for periods of time." In response, Donnelly "talked about the need to accommodate other quiet workers. I put on classical music and said, 'If you can't hear the music, then you are being too noisy for it to help you learn.'"

Donnelly's principal, Rosalie de la Cruz, said that he had been effective with black students because he made "personal connections with them and showed respect." As an example, de la Cruz recalled Donnelly's "unusual" request to have several black male students whom he'd taught the previous year reassigned to him. "They stayed on target and did well with him," she said, because "he kept them challenged."

Developing Cultural Competence as a Journey

Charles Ackerman strengthened his cultural knowledge of the modal beliefs and learning styles of black students by turning to his black friends. He mentioned that musician friends with whom he played Seattle-area soul and R&B clubs "were always telling me the 'Dos and Don'ts' of black culture. It began as we played these clubs in which I, as a white man, kind of stood out. I wasn't asking questions or anything, but they would just talk and tell me what was going on. My exposure to friends answered a lot of questions for me." For example, Ackerman recalled mentioning to his black friends that there weren't many black students in the band class he taught at school. "I thought, 'Maybe I'm doing something to turn them off,'" he said. A black friend of his suggested that although playing music was valued among blacks, playing traditional string instruments wasn't, and suggested that he start a jazz band at the school. Ackerman complied, and said the response of his black students was enthusiastic.

"I remember several black boys who played violin, but the other boys taunted them so much that they just gave it up," said Ackerman. "It just wasn't cool. I could see how they became targets. It was sad, too, because I worked hard to keep the kids in. These incidents make you think about the pressures students endure." Still, Ackerman was convinced that "it's not going to take us forever to bridge the gap. One day, we'll evolve beyond these differences. It's really important that teachers do whatever it takes to make sure that the daily experience is interesting, fun, and work-oriented, and that "kids feel that *they* are valued and *learning* something of value."

Information in Curriculum on Cultural Differences

PTP educators regularly used curriculum materials that described historical, social, and political events from a wide range of perspectives. In addition, while anchoring activities in students' ethnic, social, and cultural identities, PTP teachers acquainted students with their schools' culture, codes of power, values, beliefs, and norms and ensured that students selected their own ways of adopting them as part of their individual cultural identities.

"I work to create an authentic learning environment for students who have different racial and cultural backgrounds than I do," said middle school teacher David Maslin. "And I put black-white issues to the forefront when we're learning together. In literature, for instance, I may have my students compare the words of a black man in 1941 with those of a white man in 1920, to learn about events

from different perspectives. We address racial issues as a matter of course on a regular basis. Because our coming together to learn is a social dynamic, I can be honest and discuss differences and commonalities."

Some PTP teachers maintained unique classroom libraries filled with materials from which students could learn about events, concepts, and ideas from a variety of cultural perspectives. For example, Diana Granger maintained a rich, multicultural library in her 4th grade class that "allowed students to access their histories and see the wonderful models of achievers there—and I'm not just talking about basketball achievers. I'm talking about those people who've really worked to create a world that promotes equality, civil rights, and justice for all." Granger noted that because she and her teaching partner considered it "really important to bring in these stories all the time," they chose to spend about $2,000 on books such as "an anthology of children's literature that focused on social issues related to gender, race, war, and peace." They used those culturally relevant books and materials "as stepping stones to promote thinking" about events from varied perspectives.

Adrianne Driscoll, who taught at an all-black K–8 school, explained that even though her class "is a math and science classroom, I have a lot of books for the kids to read: collections of African American stories, as well as books on Kenya, African scientists and leaders, and mathematics in different cultures. Whenever kids are doing something for another class, they know they can always come and get a book from me. I'm like their second library."

David Maslin used culturally relevant materials and his understandings about cultural perspectives to help students understand how personal and cultural experiences influence the way individuals construct knowledge. "As a white teacher, it would be silly not to recognize how race flows through literature and surrounds us," he said. "Kids like to read and write about themselves when writing poetry and getting a handle on being a poet. When I taught mostly white kids in Idaho, I didn't think that teaching black poetry was a priority; I just used poems that I personally knew well. But now I have a personal need to teach black poets, because it helps the kids to understand their experience."

Lisa Forsythe provided opportunities for students to critique concepts learned, their origins, and their authors' economic, political, and social perspectives and motivations. "So that means not always picking things that are traditional or written by whites," she said. "Because I am a white person, and I come from that background, I try to step out of that a little bit. Often, I replace the stories in the literature book with my personal choices, or I look at the history book and flip it by finding a piece that presents the opposite side, saying, 'Whose point of view is this?' For the last three or four years, I've pointed out how easy and natural it is to see things from one point of view and taught kids that we have to try to look at concepts from multiple points of view."

At her Afrocentric school, Adrianne Driscoll made sure to share African history in an engaging, challenging way using interdisciplinary lessons and concrete representations of ideas. "For our social studies unit on ancient civilizations, the kids learned about the science and math of ancient Egypt and compared Arabic number systems to present-day systems," she said. "And when we talked about how Egyptians made mummies, *we* made mummies!" Like the other PTP educators, Driscoll found that providing factual information within culturally relevant curriculum helped to refute stereotypes and prejudices, clear up misconceptions, and increase students' sense of esteem. "These lessons inspired my students to think, 'Oh gosh, our people were really smart. I better get myself going here so that I can be as smart as they are,'" she said.

Cultural Critique and Activism

Believing that lack of engagement and voice had disadvantaged her black students in other contexts, Driscoll liked to encourage them to generate questions in class. "I don't think it's right that many black students don't ask questions because they believe others will either think 'You're stupid' or 'You're disruptive,'" she said. "I tell students, 'If you don't understand it, ask me. Please. And I will tell you.' I think that is very important for black kids, especially boys who have been told to be quiet."

Driscoll also reported actively helping students to understand and critique some of the discriminatory practices and barriers that they might encounter in life, and teaching them "strategies to get around it." She told students, "When you go to high school, you might have teachers who'll look at you and say, 'This is a black kid, he's dumb.' You're going to have to keep working to learn and show them you're smart." She felt compelled to "actually tell kids the strategies that they are going to need in life. I tell them, 'When you try to go get a job, you need to have this or that skill,' 'This is how you interview,' and 'This is how you answer a phone or speak to people in a work setting. If someone is upset with you, you need to learn not to yell and scream and get yourself fired.' I literally do all of that along with my teaching of grade-level content so that the expectations they'll encounter aren't a secret to them. It's nice for them to know that their experiences as persons of color are not a secret to me, either. "

8

Cultural Congruence in Instruction

In this chapter, we will examine how the PTP educators implemented the following strategies:

Category: Meaningful, Complex Instruction
Strategies: Teachers . . .

• Use constructivist approaches with student knowledge as the basis for inquiring, representing ideas, developing meaning, elaborating, organizing, and interacting with content.

• Teach a continuum of basic to higher-order literacy skills, knowledge, and ways of thinking to help students derive and convey meaning from text and speech, solve problems, achieve goals, develop individual knowledge and potential, and participate in society.

• Develop metacognitive skills that help children learn how to learn.

• Provide large amounts of time reading a great variety of texts.

• Engage in collaborative team teaching.

• Engage all students using meaningful, relevant, and challenging curriculum, content, and instructional activities.

• Teach concepts and skills using integrated, holistic, interdisciplinary lessons.

• Engage students in real-life, project-based contextual and vocational activities.

• Teach skills within the context of meaningful applications.

Category: Scaffolding Instruction to Home Culture and Language

Strategies: Teachers . . .

- Teach to historical, cultural, social, ethnic, and linguistic differences.
- Provide scaffolding to match or link curriculum, materials, lesson content and format, and instructional methods to students' home culture, interests, experiences, and prior learning.
- Scaffold and engage students' learning using visual images and familiar vocabulary to connect prior knowledge and new learning.
- Provide core instruction in Standard English.
- Teach academic content in preschool.

Category: Responding to Student Traits and Needs

Strategies: Teachers . . .

- Demonstrate knowledge of content.
- Understand and use speech and expressions familiar to students.
- Select and use a variety of instructional methods and interactive strategies.
- Vary strategies to meet students' motivational preferences.
- Match instructional strategies to student traits, abilities, and learning style preferences.
- Promote student use of multiple intelligences to gain, use, and respond to knowledge.
- Provide materials and learning centers for varied styles and modalities.
- Allow students to express visual, tactile, emotional, and auditory preferences.

- Incorporate student preferences for verbal expressiveness.
- Incorporate student preferences for active kinesthetic participation.
- Limit lectures to 5–10 minutes and augment them with visuals and examples.

Category: Culturally Relevant Curriculum Materials

Strategies: Teachers . . .

- Select and use culturally relevant curriculum materials from all cultural groups.
- Select and use culturally relevant visual representations of all cultural groups.
- Select and use culturally relevant books, pictures, and bulletin board items.
- Recognize culturally relevant events.
- Use manipulatives, models, artifacts, and concrete representations of concepts.
- Use primary (original) source materials.

Meaningful, Complex Instruction

The awareness and understandings that PTP educators gained as they developed their cultural competencies are essential to achieving cultural congruence in instruction (Zeichner, 1996; Knapp & Turnbull, 1991). Many researchers consider the establishment of cultural congruence to be one of three factors—along with teacher-student social interactions and attending to students' culture and developmental needs—that are essential to promoting students' cognitive development (Ladson-Billings, 2000;

Pasch, Sparks-Langer, Gardner, Starko, and Moody, 1991; Zeichner, 1996). PTP educators achieved cultural congruence by scaffolding instruction to students' backgrounds with concrete examples and models from students' lives, home culture, and language. PTP teachers and principals characterized scaffolding as a way of "leveling the playing field" for black students. Researchers observing culturally congruent classrooms found that they relied on culturally relevant texts, information, and curriculum in all subject and skills areas; used their students' home language along with textbooks; and demonstrated concepts, processes, and procedures with manipulatives, realia, and real-life contextual and vocational activities (Delpit, 2000; Gay, 2000; and Zeichner, 1996).

Constructivist Approaches

PTP educators used constructivist approaches to teaching and learning, with students engaged in group learning during meaningful, challenging, and complex tasks, interdisciplinary lessons, and project-based activities. "What is important is that you're letting all kids share in developing our knowledge," said 4th grade teacher Diana Granger. In her classroom, that meant "having students do cooperative learning, with the whole class engaged. They're talking with each other and they're sharing the learning, and we ask, 'Who wants to share their partner's brilliant thinking?' because we think being able to paraphrase is a very important skill." Granger noted that collaborative work creates greater access to learning opportunities: "If all the kids are engaged and they all have

shared their knowledge, it's not just Johnny, that one student over there raising his hand, who's able to participate and learn."

Granger maintained rigor in her class by differentiating to meet the needs of her students. "Our curriculum has been well thought out and prepared so that we can differentiate," she said. "For example, some students might be really good at their paragraph transitions, but need some instruction on literary devices," in which case she might "pull a group over to instruct them on using figurative language."

Middle school teacher Mick Denby noted that when students were involved for extended periods in group work on meaningful, challenging problems, "deep learning happens." Fourth grade teacher Chloe Gifford found that fostering this deep-level engagement required a continuous focus on "the three R's: rigor in curriculum and expectations, relevancy of content, and relationship." She also emphasized the importance of having students involved in investigations: "With whatever strand—number sense and computation, geometry, algebra—constructivism involves using investigations to develop understanding of mathematics concepts." In her class, students used transparent shapes called "seeing solids" to learn the properties of solid geometric shapes.

Higher-Order Thinking Skills

Fourth grade teacher Chloe Gifford said that she "always focused on developing as much higher-level thinking as possible" by providing a variety of oral and written communication patterns for engaging in and sharing thinking. These communication patterns, she said, included "thinking for yourself, combining thinking in pairs and groups, thinking as a classroom . . . I'm always encouraging kids to analyze and synthesize and evaluate." She recalled "always asking students, 'Why have you come to those conclusions? What's making you think that?'" as a way of unlocking potential and creativity. She said that allowing students to provide wrong answers helped her to establish "a risk-free environment" where students learned to justify their reasoning and understand that "why you picked a wrong answer is just as important as why you picked a right one." Gifford probed students to provide extended substantive oral responses—"always delving for more information, getting them to think at higher levels, and encouraging their creativity."

Middle school principal Bridget Lawley noted that teacher Susan Lansing taught students a framework for thinking through daily warm-ups consisting of exercises that encourage individual thinking, multiple responses, and diversity of thinking. Indeed, thinking-skills development is a schoolwide initiative at many PTP schools; as elementary school principal Darrell Conway noted, a "school vision that integrates multiple intelligences, technology, critical thinking, and cooperative grouping in reading, writing, and mathematics instruction is the most effective, not just for black students, but for all students."

Literacy Skills Development

PTP schools placed high priority on literacy development, with all schools taking part in the National Urban Alliance (NUA) Literacy Initiative. According to middle school teacher Michael Wagner, the initiative "was just an amazing resource for developing an understanding of urban kids in general and considering the racial and cultural issues related to what kids need." Elementary school principal Rosalie de la Cruz felt that the most valued aspects of the literacy initiative were procedures designed to help students rehearse, process, and transfer learning using a variety of methods, including direct instruction, modeling and practice strategies, mnemonics, and graphic organizers.

Wagner believed that, at the middle school level, the NUA techniques provided black students with "the support they need to independently organize their thinking. All the graphic organizers and the strategies helped them to go from 'I kind of have an idea, but I really don't get it' to 'This is where I can start. How can I structure this? How can I organize these ideas?' Over the years, we've seen great results as students developed problem-solving strategies."

According to middle school principal Alicia Baldwin, teacher Marian Katz provided "lots of minilessons on reading, particularly, nonfiction text" and "designed minilesson stations similar to what you would see in elementary classrooms" to respond to students' needs. Katz's response to students' needs aligned with findings by Cuban (1984, cited in Sleeter & Grant, 1988) showing that effective teachers of black students used student-centered activities grounded in cognitive psychology and research on brain-based learning. PTP teachers like Katz found that learning centers, individualized instruction, cooperative learning, and teacher-led instruction allowed students to attain information through varied modalities. For instance, principal de la Cruz found that Mark Donnelly met students' needs through lessons in which "kids are hearing content, vocalizing it, asking about it, and giving it back again." She noted that he used a variety of communication patterns, including "lots of back and forth," and engaged students with questioning to deepen their understanding of text.

Middle school teacher Lisa Forsythe recalled using several widely used literacy methods: "just reading as much they can, having students read independently, partner reading, and reading aloud to students every day." She also often conducted a shared reading during which she read and students followed along with text that is in front of them. Jeffrey Brooks used a variation of the shared reading method: Because his school had an open-concept plan without floor-to-ceiling walls, and to make students' voices audible to the entire class, his students would take turns reading aloud text projected onto the screen at the front of the room into a microphone.

Third grade teacher Kimberly Lazarides divided her class into ability-level groups for reading; as she pointed out, "some 3rd grade kids are reading at a 2nd grade level, and some are reading at a 6th grade level." Like Forsythe, she regularly varied how she engaged students in reading based on the purpose of the lesson and the group's ability level—reading aloud to some, reading one-on-one with others. Another 3rd grade teacher, Ryan Toth, was similarly flexible: According to his principal, Patrick Molvig, "what set him apart" was his "loose style, which suited his black students," and his ability to engage students by "giving them choices in reading and writing tasks and materials. The core of what he does is choosing interesting topics and integrating a variety of topics—sports, animals, games—with reading and writing."

Other PTP teachers opted for a more traditional approach. For example, principal Joanne Stewart found that 3rd grade teacher Mark Goldberg used accelerated learning techniques such as repetition and mnemonics to review and recall mastered material while following the district's direct instruction curriculum closely. According to his principal, Joanne Stewart, Goldberg "put a large emphasis on practicing and memorizing literature pieces, performing their recitations for the entire school, and videotaping and sending home tapes of student performances." Diana Granger, who made use of culturally responsive strategies such as call and response, also believed that repeated modeling, practice, and recitation helped "all students learn complex language and complex skills."

Many PTP teachers used journaling to help students make connections between reading and writing. Middle school teacher Carla Storey and elementary school teacher Mark Donnelly had students write in science journals to explain investigation procedures and their solutions to problems. Lisa Forsythe's students used journals to capture their Daily Oral Language (DOL) writing exercises, in which students made grammatical changes to text within the context of intact literature samples (rather than in separate sentences taken out of context).

When Forsythe's middle school students created original pieces, she led them through a process that began with journaling, included independent work, provided time for collaborative learning assistance with classmates, and culminated in their independently processing input from their teacher and peers to complete the writing task. After these preparations, Forsythe required her students to compose independently by "just working for 20 minutes, whether they're writing a rough draft or they're creating graphic organizers."

Literacy and Thinking Skills Development

Helping students learn to use information processing and metacognitive thinking skills was a strategy nearly all PTP educators supported by using the methods learned through the NUA literacy initiative, including graphic organizers. Principal Marshall Waters found that the NUA's thinking tools and graphic organizers provided "frameworks to help students formulate thinking prior to writing." At his school, he said, "The thinking maps and graphic organizers are visible on the walls in every classroom. Teachers are working on some now and will incorporate all of them over time."

According to Lisa Forsythe, the five graphic organizers used throughout her school helped create equitable access to learning opportunities for all students. "They opened the playing field for every kid to have an opportunity to organize information in a way that made sense to them," she said. "For example, recently I had the kids select one of the five

organizers to complete a visual aid for their book report. Even my kids who struggle in some areas of their learning created visual aids that were of the same or even better quality than those made by kids who do great work all the time. There's something about that graphic organizer that 'equals it out' for kids from all different backgrounds."

Third grade teacher Glen Roberts explained how graphic organizers aided his students' thinking during their study of a fiction book they were reading in class. Roberts had students use the Venn diagram organizer to analyze two of the main characters in the book. He noted that the images in graphic organizers helped with students' thinking. "In a multiformat, you have your event in the middle, the causes before, and the effects after. You can see how one event leads to another. You can see how the mind works. All these graphics illustrate the thinking that we do all the time. Pretty soon, students are starting to generalize and can see cause and effect on their own, and how that dynamic might occur in something else we might have read." In addition, Roberts found that tools such as sequencing flow maps allowed "some kids who are better with drawing to construct a picture representing the story's actions."

Roberts also used the Synonym Triplets strategy, a variation of call-and-response, to help strengthen vocabulary. For example, he helped his class learn synonyms for the word "proud" by calling out two synonyms to students. The students' response was to call back the two words in a rhythmic way: "I'm proud, I'm AR-ro-gant!" In the next round, Roberts called out the word "conceited," to which students responded with a rhythmic cheer and pumping hand gestures: "I'm proud! I'm arrogant! I'm conceited!" As Roberts noted, "the rhythm and the action aid recall."

Marshall Waters found that the NUA strategies and tools aimed at vocabulary building supported black students "who come with deficiencies in language and vocabulary. For instance, we use taxonomies, Word Wall, rap, songs, and rhymes. Word Wall involves making the vocabulary we are teaching and learning prominent by putting the words on the walls. In that way, everyone can build on them and revisit them often to understand them. We also use Dancing Definitions, where our K–5 teachers have the students take a definition and change it into a jingle. For instance, take the phrase 'A sailor is a person who sails across the sea.' When you ask a student, 'What is a sailor?' he might say, 'Ah, ah, ah, ah a sailor is, a sailor is / a sailor is a person / a sailor is a person who sails across the sea / sails across the sea / sails across the sea.' By putting the definition to song, it makes it easier to access memory and meaning and build vocabulary."

In addition to the NUA methods and tools, PTP teachers used trade programs and state curriculum resources to assist with literacy development. Chloe Gifford, for example, used the Word Market program "for several science and math concepts." She explained that the program helped students make connections in text while involving them "in finding, learning, and competing with peers both here at school and in other schools to share larger and larger stores of vocabulary words. Anytime I'd say a word or they came across a new word in their reading, students added those to their cache of Word Market word cards. I'm always trying to find ways for them to use the words they have in Word Market so that they can *take ownership* of the words."

Scaffolding Instruction to Home Culture and Language

Relevance to students' culture was one of the key features that middle school teacher Moira Reynolds considered when determining how to teach content. "With any subject-area reading, the main issues are, 'How does it connect with the students' lives? How does it impact them personally?'" she said. To help students make personal and meaningful connections to historical content, Reynolds had students "journal daily on something we're studying in history, but adding references that connect with their lives." Similarly, principal de la Cruz found that even with a direct instruction curriculum, Mark Donnelly was able to "pull in experiences and make sure kids were connecting using information about themselves and their families." Principal Kim Hanh Nguyen noted that Jessica Wakefield also tended to scaffold her students' learning by connecting prior knowledge to current lessons. "She relates things back to what they learned before," she said. "She will say, 'Remember when your assignment was to observe bubbles rising in the water when you boiled eggs at home?' She provides modeling and cognitive scaffolding, making analogies and connections for the kids and asks them to make the connections as well."

Mick Denby found it "interesting to talk about how math is related to things students encounter outside school." By allowing students to share their stories of personal experiences with math outside the classroom, he was able to incorporate their preference for verbal expressiveness and "relates whatever we are doing in class to what is going on in life." Denby recalled allowing students to share their experiences soliciting pledges for the school walk-a-thon as a way to help them draw analogies to the study of linear relations. "We had this problem about three students traveling at different rates and deciding how much they'd make from pledges. Students were engaged, talking about pledging, saying, 'I did that.' We then graphed this problem in which three people wanted to charge different rates." Denby noted that this kind of in-depth consideration of one problem to which students could relate benefited them more than "just covering 20 problems" by responding to their motivational needs. "If there's discussion, it's time well spent because they are motivated," he said.

For Angela Chaffee, scaffolding meant maintaining excitement and enthusiasm in the classroom by "making sure kids understand what you're attempting to teach." She said that "to get kids hooked," she would vary the level of abstraction in course content, presenting it first in "ways that they could understand it and grab it" and then progressively increasing the level of abstraction, "moving it up as they are able to understand it." She stressed that her goal was "for them to improve and to learn. My adjusting the curriculum and materials provides scaffolding between where kids are and where you want them to be." Chaffee was firmly convinced that "starting out where they are and then bringing them up, little by little, helps kids to

improve and love learning. I've learned that if you're talking above kids' heads, they're never going to learn anything, and their reaction is to become a discipline problem."

Demonstrating Teacher Skill and Knowledge of Content

PTP educators felt that maintaining an extensive repertoire of pedagogical skills and knowledge was at the heart of their ability to respond to students' traits and needs. In a comprehensive review of studies carried out over a 20-year period in varied settings and demographic groups, Arroyo, Rhoad, and Drew (1999) found that the most important influences on student achievement related to teachers' skills, knowledge, and professional behaviors. Stronge (2002) found that the key trait of effective teachers is the ability to apply knowledge or skills to particular populations or settings. According to both Pasch and colleagues (1991) and Irvine and Armento (2001), teacher content knowledge and reflective pedagogical practices are inextricably linked. Ladson-Billings's research on successful teachers of black students revealed that the three key elements of their practice were "high expectations for all students, cultural congruence in instruction, and teacher content knowledge and a variety of teaching strategies" (1994, p. 57).

PTP educators acquired content knowledge and developed their pedagogical practice through a variety of methods. Jessica Wakefield had a master's degree in technology; Charles Ackerman participated in study groups with other teachers, conducting "a lot of research on their practices"; Jeffrey Brooks personally conducted research on "the test scores of all the schools in the state" and contacted teachers "in schools that did well to ask, 'What are you doing to be so successful?'"; and Darrell Conway had conducted doctoral research on ethnic differences, multiple intelligences, and the demographic differences between teachers and public school students.

Varying Strategies to Meet Students' Learning Styles

According to Durodoyle and Hildreth (1995), researchers have found that the following instructional strategies are particularly advantageous to black students: an openness to oral expressiveness, stylistic creativity, and adaptability; cooperative learning activities; discussion; hands-on work; whole-to-part learning; practical and relevant application of learning; and attention to the salience of nonverbal communication, movement, and rhythm. When PTP teachers spoke of their processes for selecting and applying a variety of instructional strategies, they demonstrated their sensitivity to students' developmental needs and differences. Kimberly Lazarides noted that she found what worked with her students because she "really make a conscious effort to think about" how her students differed. "I definitely think that realizing students' different needs, regardless of skin color, and realizing that the same strategies won't work with all kids, has helped," she said.

Having a broad repertoire of strategies is useless unless teachers demonstrate the flexibility to use them when needed. Angela Chaffee used her students' reactions as the gauge by which to judge the effectiveness of her lessons. When she incorporated activities in response to students' learning style preferences, she often asked for students' feedback on the effectiveness of her efforts. "I ask the kids, 'Does this help you when I'm writing on the board? Does it help to speak? Does it help when I show things on the overhead?' When they respond with a resounding 'Yes!' that's what I do."

"Black kids are just like any other kids," said Chloe Gifford. "They need variety and different ways of engaging and learning. Everybody's different. If we say, 'They all move around a lot,' well, they don't. It's kind of racist to think that." Gifford pointed out that she made variations to meet different learning styles, "especially if it's an introduction to a lesson. I'm visual, so I will often use the overhead." She said that she helped students understand why she varied strategies by "telling the kids that a learning style is a specific strength in how you take in information."

Danielle Kaplan emphasized that awareness of her verbal linguistic strengths drove her to "go out of my way to have kids show their learning in other ways. They can draw, write, or sing on assignments and assessments." For example, Owen Callahan observed Jeffrey Brooks engaging auditory learners by reading historical fiction aloud, and kinesthetic learners by lining them up to demonstrate factors and multiples in math. In addition, Brooks promoted active learning by having the students "hear the Jewish special education assistant and the 1st grade teacher's dad share stories of the effects of the Holocaust on kids and having the kids exchange letters with dads who are serving in the Iraq War."

Responding to Preferences for Verbal Expressiveness, Music, and Kinesthetic Engagement

PTP educators understood that, in constructivist classrooms, dialogue among teachers and students supports cognitive development and a deeper understanding of content. Teachers Michael Wagner, Jeffrey Brooks, and Chloe Gifford all used the exact same words to describe their black students: "they like to talk." Brooks observed that "what I see culturally, being a black male myself, is that we have a need to express ourselves more. So in group work, we get to do that." According to Gifford, "black students use more verbal techniques and animation, perhaps because of the power that is conferred with 'being able to speak out.'"

Moira Reynolds recalled that many of her black students "loved to have the opportunity to write music or perform a skit as opposed to just writing a five-paragraph essay." Like other PTP teachers, Reynolds engaged her students in dialogue prior to reading and writing. In addition, she "used short audio or video clips" to provide concrete representations of concepts and motivate students to write. "The kids love those little snippets I use," she said. "They're super engaging for all my middle school kids, including my black kids." She recalled that when she limited the length of lectures and augmented them with visuals, students "remembered so much more than if I had just talked for 20 minutes."

Ryan Toth noted that he "would wait a while, and then let the kids talk" after posing questions in class. "I try to give students as much voice as possible when we talk in the beginning," he said. "They need to talk it out. We did a lot of brainstorming, and I would fill the board with their ideas before even setting a challenge for them."

In addition to using oral discourse prior to reading and writing, Adrianne Driscoll incorporated music and movement in her lessons—a strategy that Delpit (2000) found was often evident in effective and culturally responsive classrooms. Marshall Waters, the principal at Driscoll's school, noted that she "used movement, music, and songs throughout her teaching" to accelerate learning by helping students rehearse and transfer information to long-term memory.

"At our school, we emphasize that all things have rhythm and patterns, whether it's songs, words, good writing, or bad writing," continued Waters. "Our scholars learn strategies to find those patterns. Prior to writing an essay, we take a piece of writing apart and discuss its parts. We dissect good sentences to find their subjects and verbs, and we discuss how to make them better, expand them, and extend them on what we call a 'sentence stretcher.'"

Charles Ackerman recalled opening each math class with "music that played while kids did their warm-up problems. In my band classes, I played music and we'd talk about the composer." To make interdisciplinary connections between math and music, he said, he would "put the composer's years of birth and death up and ask the kids, 'How old is or was the composer?' Then, we'd talk about the composer's time period: 'What do we know about what happened during the composer's life?'" Ackerman also made sure to use culturally relevant content and materials from many cultural groups. "I developed a kind of schedule to help with varying it all the time," he said, "so that I selected music from not only Europe, but from China, Japan, South America, Cuba, or Africa."

Carla Storey said she used "creative ways to teach" that integrated students' preferences for active engagement, collaborative learning, and excitement to balance daily routines and rituals. Essentially, her weekly games became classroom rituals. "In addition to our school-wide adoption of the Word Wall to strengthen vocabulary, we use games like Bongo and Word Snatch that allow students to learn vocabulary," she said. "For instance, in Word Snatch, someone gives a definition and kids run to 'snatch' the word and use it in context. My classes include special education kids and English language learners, and these games address different learning styles."

As Chloe Gifford noted, teachers who know their students' backgrounds develop "a sense of what kids like to do." Gillian Novak said she found that helping students "to look for their learning style gift and feeding into that gift" was highly motivating for students. She recalled "one black boy whose interest came alive as we composed poetry on a field trip to the zoo."

Culturally Relevant Curriculum Materials

Diana Granger offered an example of her emphasis on culturally relevant curriculum materials. One day, as she and a young black female student named Ebony were considering the books available at a school book fair,

Ebony disclosed that she couldn't afford to buy a book. Granger, who felt strongly about promoting collectiveness and collaboration, suggested that the two of them look at books together "and see if we can find one to buy for the classroom." Granger recalled being pleased that Ebony, who read at a 3rd grade level but was in the 5th grade, chose the book *Think Again* by the rapper Doug E. Fresh. She suggested that Ebony use the book to develop a rap and teach it to the whole class. "By God, she had this long rap memorized in a week," said Granger. The assignment engaged Ebony's musical intelligence while also improving her reading ability. "It was incredible," Granger enthused. "She demonstrated what some researchers say: that 90 percent of what you teach, you learn. Her reading has just skyrocketed this year. She's not quite at 5th grade standard yet, but she has come up almost two years. I attribute her success to just taking that moment to see her connection to this music and this little rap book and supporting her as she just took the assignment and ran with it. We performed the rap for the whole school during our Martin Luther King Jr. Day assembly, and it was incredible!"

At a later point, Ebony came to Granger with a different book she was reading and said, "You know, Diana, I noticed that you could rhyme this book out. It's not a poem, but you could rap it out." Granger believed that she "had internalized the rhythm of language in a way that was really incredible. That's how you use the multiple intelligences. You just have to find those moments when you can use the intelligences to change students' learning in a really deep way."

Meaningful, Relevant, and Challenging Curriculum and Project-Based Learning

PTP teachers engaged students using meaningful, relevant, and challenging curriculum and project-based learning activities featuring active, hands-on problem solving and manipulatives. For example, Danielle Kaplan had her students conduct simulations in which they took on the roles of city planners. Her students each chose a city to focus on, conducted in-depth research on what contributed to its sustainability, and presented their reports to the class. "Deadlines are spaced out to make it manageable," said Kaplan. "The kids like it because they get to move around and talk. Students find it more engaging than just sitting, reading, and writing."

To help students conceptualize abstract ideas, Susan Lansing used what she referred to as an "unconventional modeling technique: I do visualization of 3D objects with my students. Since some kids haven't done that before," she said, they find the technique highly motivational. Lansing and other math teachers at her school also conducted what they called "a celebration of learning" about *pi,* during which 7th graders faced off against administrators in a contest to remember as many digits of *pi* ($\pi = 3.14159 \ldots$) as possible. As part of the celebration, Lansing served pie to her students in class.

Mark Donnelly used a project in which students constructed a model of a 19th-century town to deepen students' understanding of the concepts of perspective and vanishing point. He first illustrated the concepts by having students watch their classmates' heights diminish as they walked down the hallway. For another project, Donnelly took his students outside to plan and build a fence around a patch of school ground. As they worked, Donnelly shared with his students that he was also building a fence at his new house, reminding them that "they were getting training in a real life experience: 'Gang, you're doing what I had to do to figure it out.'"

A Virtual Walk through Mark Donnelly's 4th Grade Class

The pastel-colored hallways outside Mark Donnelly's 4th grade classroom are arrayed with students' writing and social studies work samples. On this June day, Donnelly, who is dressed in blue jeans and a Hawaiian shirt, speaks to the class in the quiet, even voice that his principal touts as one of the characteristics that make him so effective teaching black students. He draws the attention of his diverse student group to the screen at the front of the room, on which he has projected a perspective drawing of a hallway. Students sit in pairs at tables facing the front of the room or forming a horseshoe along three walls. The classroom is brightly lit, orderly, and well-organized. The walkthrough teams observe storage cubbies in the background and posters featuring root words alongside colorful samples of student work on the walls.

Although the students are quiet and attentive as Donnelly begins the lesson, they wave their hands and crow, "Ooh! Ooh!" when he poses a question. Students are clearly interested in what they are learning and in the activities related to their class project:

creating a replica of an 18th-century town. Using a constructivist approach to learning, Donnelly begins his lesson by saying, "We are going to talk about perspective." He immediately encourages students to draw on their prior knowledge by asking, "What do you think of the word *spec*?" When several students respond "spectacles," Donnelly asks them to elaborate on their thinking by asking, "So what do you use spectacles for?"

Mahari, a black boy seated near the front of the room, exclaims, "Oh, I know. They help you see." This answer begins an exchange during which several students offer similar ideas. With students saying "I know, I know" in the background, and Donnelly making eyeglasses shapes with his hands in front of his eyes, he agrees: "Right, they help you see." Using hand gestures to accentuate each syllable and provide a model of his ideas, Donnelly repeats, "So, *per-spec-tive*. What does *per-spec-tive* mean?" The question is met with multiple suggestions and raised hands. One student cries out, "Ooh! Ooh! It makes you see *better*."

Donnelly, sitting on a stool next to the projector, repeats the student's answer: "It makes you see *better*. Well, kind of." When another student offers that perspective "makes me think of a drawing," Donnelly repeats his statement and asks for "a couple more tries." Several students raise their hands. Donnelly calls on one, a young black boy named Kyle, who answers: "When you draw a picture, it helps you visualize the thing that you're drawing."

Seated like Rodin's *The Thinker*, Donnelly fields students' responses and helps them draw out their prior knowledge. "Hmm, that's pretty close," he says to Kyle, then begins to explain to the class how painters frame a perspective of whatever it is they anticipate painting. He draws on his knowledge of the students' traits and background in his classroom as he explains the concept of framing:

"Some of you like to paint, right? In the olden days, if you were a painter and you were commissioned—that means you were paid—to paint a building in Seattle or right here in front of our school, you would stand somewhere where you could get a nice view of the building." Donnelly backs up and forms a square shape with his hands. "You would stand back like this and look through your hands, like this. That's called framing." He moves around, demonstrating his "frame" in front of several students' desks, and continues: "What's in that frame is what you're going to see; it's called your *perspective*." Several students can be observed making frames with their own hands. "I don't care about anything other than what's through my hands—that's what I'm interested in," says Donnelly. At a table near the door, the teacher assistant and several students look at each other through their "frames" and smile.

Describing the task for the day, Donnelly tells students that they will be using a technique similar to that used in moviemaking, in which artists use computer software to generate special effects that make things look "really giant or like they're a long ways away when in fact the audience is looking at a flat screen." Here he points at the overhead screen, and several students begin chattering about computers and special effects. Donnelly gains their attention again, telling them that while they "don't have the fancy computer equipment to do what the moviemakers do," he will teach them "a really simple method that I learned in a book and practiced." He portrays himself as a lifelong learner who is willing to share what he learns with students. "Believe it or not, people couldn't figure out how to capture perspective in paintings for thousands of years—until about the 14th century."

Several students chatter quietly as Donnelly moves to the supplies table in the center of the room. Placing a film on the overhead projector lens, Donnelly says, "After I show you this picture, we're going to go stand in the hall." He makes a frame with his hands. "The hall is so long, you can get a good sense of visual perspective looking down it. Then, when we come back in, you're going to practice making a perspective drawing." Kyle has silently moved over to stand by the door and listen to this demonstration. Donnelly allows students to stand or sit, as long as they're paying attention.

Donnelly projects four vocabulary words associated with the day's lesson onto the screen: *facade, horizon line, vanishing point,* and *construction line.* Students eagerly attempt to pronounce *facade* as soon as it is shown, but all pronounce it *fa-kade.* Donnelly corrects them, sharing the word's origin: "It looks like *fa-kade,* but it's a French word—*facade.* Everybody say it: *facade.*" Again drawing on students' prior knowledge, Donnelly asks them if they know what the word means. After fielding a few incorrect responses, he asks if anyone has ever seen a Western movie being made. One student yells out, "Old Winthrop, Washington!" Donnelly explains: "If moviemakers need to show the Winthrop hotel, they wouldn't necessarily film the actual hotel; they might just have a

re-creation of the front of it. It looks like the hotel on camera, but it's really just the front—like the face, the *facade.* Try *facade* again." After the students repeat the term, Donnelly lets them know that they will be making facades of their buildings.

Using repetition and choral response, Donnelly introduces the other three words on the screen. Assuring students that they will be given written directions for how to make a perspective drawing, he invites them to come with him into the hall to "get just a feel for what it looks like to look down a tunnel." When he announces that he will "have a volunteer go way down to the greenhouse and we'll see how small they get," several students yell out at once: "I'll do it! I'll do it!"

In the hallway, some members of the class sit on the floor and others stand before large picture windows. Demonstrating his familiarity with students, Donnelly places his hand on a student named Tran and explains: "Tran is going to go down to the greenhouse down there and we're going to see how small he's going to get." Showing their interest in what is going on in class, several students imitate Donnelly as he frames Tran's head with his hands and explains, "Sometimes the distance between your fingers can seem like the size of his head." Gesturing with his hands, he continues: "Look at the lines on each side of the hall where the wall meets the floor—they seem to almost rise and go up the further down the hall you go."

Next, Donnelly directs Tran to start walking away, noting to the class that "he's shrinking." Thoroughly enjoying themselves and laughing, the students measure Tran's height with their fingers as he recedes, and some frame him with their hands. Donnelly explains how the lines of the hallway converge at a virtual vanishing point. The entire class yells for Tran to "Stop!" Donnelly repeats how small Tran's head appears to have gotten and how all the lines in the hall appear to have converged at a point. He asks Tran to walk in the middle of the hall so that the class can gauge his increase in size as he returns. When Tran is back with the group, the students spontaneously applaud. Donnelly lets them know that when they go inside, they are to begin by drawing on scratch paper, starting with their horizon line.

As students return to the classroom, most of them are smiling, and some are singing softly. They begin working on their individual perspective drawings, offering each other advice on technique. Donnelly circulates around the room commenting on work. "Does that look like you're looking down a tunnel?" he asks one student. He kneels before the desk of Terrell, a black boy seated as one of a table pair near the window. Donnelly points to his drawing, offering advice on erasing some of the lines he has drawn. As he backs away from the table, he collides with Kyle, who is walking behind him. In keeping with the class practice of treating each other with civility, Donnelly and Kyle apologize to each other, and Donnelly lightly touches Kyle's shoulder. Moving on to a nearby table, Donnelly makes a quick assessment and offers advice about the students' work.

Donnelly alternates between conferring with students individually or in small groups and talking to the class as a whole group. Students react positively to the challenge of the activity, continually asking questions of Donnelly and the teacher assistant. Donnelly provides scaffolding to match students' prior experience using familiar vocabulary, commends their efforts ("These drawings are amazing"), and promotes practice to attain mastery through modeling and guided practice. "Go ahead, once you get that line, try one more time," he says. "That's why this is a practice sheet. In order to get a flat front of the building, you erase these lines; look at your blue sheet if you're a little confused, that will help you. If you're totally stumped, just flip the paper over and try again. This is practice."

Four students finish their drawings around the same time, and one of them asks, "So Mr. Donnelly, what if we're done? What are we supposed to do now?" Donnelly challenges them to "practice drawing windows. Windows are kind of tricky because they come to an angle and are parallel to the perspective lines." One student is having trouble with her drawing, so he probes to ensure that she is getting the assistance she needs: "Any questions? Need some help?" She asks him, "Mr. Donnelly, why do I always have this? Can I take this down?" Donnelly reviews her work. "Okay, what you have here is a construction line," he says. "Now you can keep this here and you'll have a window, but this line turns into a sidewalk." Satisfied with his support, the student responds, "Cool."

Donnelly continues to circulate around the classroom, assessing students' progress while guiding them to supplies, reminding them that they can use rulers, suggesting ways to approach their work ("Visualize first, then draw"), and encouraging them to self-assess. Students enjoy the climate of collaboration and challenge presented in the lesson.

"Boys and girls, you don't have to worry about your drawings looking like something an architect might draw," says Donnelly as the observers prepare to leave the room. "We're learning, so if your drawing is a little off, don't worry about it. All architects did just as you're doing today once, struggling away. They weren't coming up with beautiful drawings from the beginning." At one table, Donnelly commends the students' work: "You may not think that it's beautiful, but I do." At another, he says, "Don't worry about it, just get used to the technique and have a good time." Coaxing the students to assume the role of authentic practitioners, he encourages them: "Boys and girls, you're artists! Let's see you take different perspectives as you work. I want to show you a technique that Juan and I discussed for creating shadows. . . ."

Walkthrough Wrap-Up

Before convening in the teachers' workroom for a facilitated feedback session, the walkthrough team gathers in the hallway outside Donnelly's classroom, taking a few minutes to make checks next to strategies that team members observed on their individual feedback forms and to add to the notes they made. Then, the observers each share the notes that they wrote at the bottom of their forms, in the section titled "What Teachers/Students Say/Do Related to the Focus Area." Here's what the teachers found:

Teacher 1
Teacher 1 found that Donnelly provided meaningful, complex instruction; scaffolded instruction to meet students' learning styles, cultural traits, and needs; used culturally relevant curriculum and materials; promoted kinesthetic participation; and fully engaged all students in demonstrating concepts. Because Donnelly had students actively participate in processing information, Teacher 1 thought that the students were likely to develop full and deep understandings of the concept of perspective in drawing. She also noted that Donnelly used a constructivist approach to learning the new concept by introducing the topic to the class and then immediately encouraging students' responses to help discern their prior knowledge ("What do you think of the word *spec*?").

Teacher 2
Teacher 2 was particularly drawn to Donnelly's strategies for enhancing students' literacy skills. He found it noteworthy that after validating students' suggestions on the meaning of perspective, Donnelly went on to use hand gestures and visuals to help students understand the lesson. Teacher 2 also noted that Donnelly used repetition and choral response to help students learn vocabulary terms.

Teacher 3
Teacher 3 observed that prior to taking the students into the hallway, Donnelly made the connection between the visual model he had displayed for the class and what the students were going to see in the hallway. Then, after assuring the students that they would be given written directions for how to make a perspective drawing, he invited them to "get a feel for what it's like to look down a tunnel."

Teacher 3 also noted that Donnelly actively engaged his students in the concrete representation of perspective by having Tran walk away and then back to the group.

Teacher 4

Teacher 4 noted that Donnelly's students clearly enjoyed the hallway demonstration, applauding Tran when he returned to the group. She also noted that they applied what they had seen in the demonstration as they worked on their individual perspective drawings. Consistent with the collaborative approach to learning that Donnelly had fostered, students offered advice to one another on drawing technique. Teacher 4 also observed that Donnelly provided modeling and guided practice and enthusiastically commended their practice to attain mastery ("These drawings are amazing!").

9

Cooperative Group Instruction

In this chapter, we will examine how the PTP educators implemented the following strategies:

Category: Group Environment and Composition

Strategies: Teachers . . .

• Structure environments to allow for cooperative learning and group activities.

• Create flexible student groupings.

• Balance familiar and unfamiliar group members when structuring groups.

• Create low-high mixed dyads to enhance achievement for students.

• Regularly place students in groups mixed by race, gender, and ability.

• Balance facilitated student learning with teacher-centered whole-class presentations.

Category: Student Collaboration and Efficacy Development

Strategies: Teachers . . .

• Promote a group-centered collaborative approach toward learning.

• Honor students' preference for cohesive group participation when formatting lessons.

• Promote student-to-student assistance for most learning tasks.

• Use a variety of oral and written communication patterns, including pair, team, and whole-class responses following collaborative work.

- Ensure that tasks are doable and group goals are attainable.
- Ensure that students understand individual roles in content mastery and task completion.
- Ensure that all students in groups share important roles and demonstrate their expertise during small-group tasks.
- Scaffold learning and gradually transfer responsibility to students, teaching students to self-monitor skills and knowledge development.
- Provide scaffolding through reciprocal teaching in which students gradually assume the role of teacher, helping their peers with learning tasks.
- Provide instruction and practice in comprehension strategies such as predicting, generating questions, clarifying, and summarizing using authentic texts.

Group Environment and Composition

Cooperative group instruction and collaborative learning strategies allow effective and culturally responsive teachers to build lesson formats on students' preference for cohesive group participation. Although variations exist among students and between teachers and students who share similar ethnic heritages, research over decades has indicated that many black students' learning styles include preferences for cooperative activities, tactile and kinesthetic processing during learning, interactions focused on people and verbal interactions, and proficiency in nonverbal communications (Eberly College of Arts & Sciences, West Virginia University, n.d.; Hill,

1999). After assessing her students' learning styles and interaction patterns, Adrianne Driscoll said that she organized students according to shared traits "because I want to have groups of kids where everybody can contribute something" and share problem-solving expertise. Similarly, 3rd grade teacher Ryan Toth "worked hard to group kids together who get along." Middle school teacher Kevin Friedman reported that he regularly used "the results of skills assessments to group together all those having the same problems." Jeffrey Brooks acknowledged that while "there're some pros and cons to ability-based groups," on the whole he thought the approach worked. He and his team partner alternated teaching their ability-grouped math and reading students. "We do this because it allows us to meet the kids at their level of need," he said.

In addition to focusing attention on the composition of groups, PTP teachers did their best to balance facilitated student learning with teacher-centered presentations to the whole class. Middle school teacher Michael Wagner found that when students are engaged in learning activities, his job as "teacher was just to guide them." According to elementary school principal Mai Pham, teacher Glen Roberts allowed his students to "wonder on their own with his guidance to make decisions and develop solutions."

Student Collaboration and Efficacy Development

Third grade teacher Donna Schneider asserted that "cooperative group learning involves kids in a community way of learning" that she felt was "obviously better than working alone." Schneider believed that emphasizing strong social interactions and a sense of community in the classroom promoted positive student relations that helped students learn from each other. Ryan Toth concurred. "Some of the students would just prefer to sit one on one, but in my view, group work is such an important a part of education," he said. "There is a social aspect to my classroom; I don't want anybody just working in isolation. We have to be part of a group." To foster the cohesiveness necessary for productive collaboration, Toth started each school year by having his students share personal stories and family histories with the class.

Middle school principal Alicia Baldwin saw Michael Wagner working to change the dynamics in his mathematics classroom "from a highly competitive nature to a real inclusive nature. He emphasizes that everybody is important. All ideas are good. When solving problems, two heads are better than one." She noted that during group discussions in Wagner's class, "the kids are participating; they're raising their hands."

Honoring Students' Preference for Cohesive Group Participation When Formatting Lessons

Ryan Toth found small-group work uniquely effective with black students. "These kids definitely profit from the small groups," he said. "They really like the interactions with other students. They like to discuss what they're doing while they complete the steps in a task. I often feel that my job as a teacher is just to guide them." Elementary school teacher Diana Granger stated that she "had

students work in groups so that they learn to trust each other in their learning." As in other constructivist classrooms, Granger set the stage for students to develop understanding by promoting participation and dialogue among group members. "When they're talking with each other, responding when I say, 'Share your partner's brilliant thinking,' all kids are sharing in developing knowledge," she said. Principal Naira Peet found that 6th grade teacher Danielle Kaplan used norms for small-group interactions to build a sense of community in the classroom and teach students human dignity principles of civility, patience, and support. "No one insults or puts down another," she said. "If students don't participate, they are not told, 'You're dumb because you didn't participate.'"

Ensuring that Students Understand Their Roles and Responsibilities for Content Mastery and Task Completion

In middle school teacher David Maslin's classroom, principal Kim Hanh Nguyen saw students helping each other get organized for group work, finding materials, and, once engaged in group work, holding each other responsible for learning content and meeting standards. Ryan Toth noted that to help his students support each other in learning content, he taught them scaffolding techniques such as how to ask probing questions, offer hints and clues, and demonstrate procedures before seeking his help. Reciprocal teaching of this sort proved particularly effective with black students. As Alicia Baldwin noted, allowing "kids to be the experts, to be the teachers, definitely works with black students." Middle school teacher Carla Storey noted that her black students especially relished "the responsibility" aspect of reciprocal teaching.

Middle school teacher Berkeley McGuire uses reciprocal teaching for reading instruction in her class with student groups of five, employing a strategy that she refined over the years with a district reading specialist. "It's really cool!" she said. "There are four parts. Kids read individually, then again in groups, at which time the group members perform their roles. The Clarifier points out and asks the group if there are ideas that need clarifying. They take notes throughout the process and use the dictionary right away. The Questioner asks 'the five Ws and H'—who, what, when, where, why, how—about the reading and solicits other questions. The Predictor makes 'I wonder if . . .'" statements and predicts what he or she thinks will come next in the reading. The Summarizer presents the most important ideas within the selection." Students rotate the roles so that each gets a chance to perform each role over time. One of McGuire's colleagues told her that as a result of her instruction using reciprocal teaching, "her kids came to social studies classes knowing how to write" narrative and expository papers.

A Virtual Walk through Adrian Driscoll's 6th Grade Science Lesson

The Afrocentric physical, conceptual, and curricular design of Adrianne Driscoll's K–8

school distinguishes it from the other 78 elementary schools in the Seattle school district. The school features a 90-seat lecture hall, a cafeteria, and a gymnasium with a stage. According to the school's website, its "African-centered curriculum recognizes that humanity started in Africa and emphasizes the history, culture, and heritage of Africans and African Americans through an interdisciplinary approach." The school emphasizes understanding the effect of cultural experiences on how students construct knowledge. School staff and students show mutual and genuine respect for cultural pride and diversity. Each class in the school adopts a different historically black U.S. college or university, with which it develops a relationship. Ninety-one percent of the school's students are black.

When the five teachers in the walkthrough team enter Driscoll's class, they find it bustling and alive with the chatter of students returning from an electives class. The students are all dressed in variations of the school uniform—hunter green cardigan, jumper, white shirt, and plaid skirt or black pants. Some of the students walk past a table arrayed with supplies for the day's science lesson as they head to their tables, where they sit in groups of three to five. Driscoll, a tall blonde in her 30s, speaks in a booming, energetic voice as she explains that today students will conduct a variety of science experiments in which they will identify the traits of two pollutants, black pepper and malachite, in the water supply of an imaginary city. This lesson is designed to engage all students through meaningful, relevant, and challenging content and activities.

Driscoll begins the class by explaining how students will use a Venn diagram graphic organizer to represent ideas as they perform the experiments outlined in their lab books. The students will be asked to describe the outcomes of their tests to understand the similarities and differences in the ways the two pollutants react with water. Driscoll's students have already had extensive practice completing science performance tasks grounded in authentic scenarios that match the format and processes used in statewide assessments, and they have also used the Venn diagram graphic organizer in multiple previous lessons.

Students listen attentively as Driscoll commends James for raising his hand to volunteer and has him tell the class the purpose of the day's experiments. Some students begin to chatter as Driscoll reviews safety procedures and explains the reciprocal teaching roles that students must play: some reading directions, some picking up racks of supplies and goggles, and some checking the progress of the work. Driscoll has built the lesson format on her students' preference for cohesive group participation.

After telling table representatives (or "getters") to pick up their eye droppers, magnifying glasses, plastic cups of water, goggles, and plastic trays, Driscoll begins to circulate around the room. The getters form a line at the supplies table and then take the equipment to their groups. Meanwhile, Driscoll follows up on her opening directions by engaging in individual conversations with each of the nine table groups. Smiling, she stops her circuit of the room to make sure that groups focus on

the appropriate lab report and then reminds the students that their work will be easier if they use the flow map graphic organizer on a specific page of their lab books to help them remember the order of the procedures in the experiments.

Within a few seconds, the noise level in the classroom becomes very high, but students are clearly working. They are intrigued by their investigations and freely move about the room, talking to their table partners and those in nearby groups to help each other complete their tasks. Donning their goggles, students lift one-inch cylinders of pepper and malachite to examine their traits. From time to time, Driscoll reminds the entire class, "Everybody in the group needs to make that double-bubble map of similarities and differences." At various tables, she offers prompts, makes inquiries, or asks questions to guide the students' procedures or thinking. Her continuous, frequent assessments allow her to determine students' skills and knowledge, provide feedback on goals attainment, and create interventions.

At a table in the center of the room, two partners are counting the seconds as they stir the pollutants in the water: "One, one-thousand; two, one-thousand; three, one-thousand." Stopping at a table near the front of the room, Driscoll cautions Shakir, a wiry young man, to set his chair on all four legs, providing corrective advice on appropriate behavior (not to mention preventing a potential accident). Then, she lays her hands on Rani's shoulders and asks him how he is doing. When Rani responds that he's ready for the next experiment, Driscoll explains the directions for a new task.

Dyonnie, wearing her goggles atop her head, walks up to Driscoll, taps her on the arm, and asks how she should record her data. Driscoll and her students are clearly at ease with each other, and she is personally inviting and accessible to students. Back at her table, Dyonnie rejoins her partner Sasha to collaborate on describing what they observed after stirring the pollutants into their cup. Like other students in Driscoll's class, Dyonnie and Sasha use prior knowledge as the basis for inquiry, representing ideas, developing meaning, and interacting with content. They agree that both substances float and record this in their lab notes, after which Dyonnie reports and records that malachite stinks. Tyson, the third member of the table group, walks over, picks up the cup of water, and shouts, "There's something in our water! It's floatin' around!" Having internalized the role of task manager, Sasha warns him to "stop playing." Wringing his hands, he continues: "Don't you see that? It *looked* like a spider." Continuing with the task, Sasha reports, "Okay, they're both types of powder."

Tiana comes over from the next table to get Dyonnie's help in adjusting the headband on her goggles. Meanwhile, Driscoll again reminds the whole class to "fill in the double bubble with likenesses and differences." At a table near the front of the room, April tells her partner Neveah that she has just done that. After a quick look at her report, Neveah replies, "N-N-N-No, you didn't." "Yes, I did," replies April; "N-N-N-No, you didn't," repeats Neveah. They go back and forth like this a

few times, until Neveah peers at her partner's lab report and begins to discuss the similarities and differences that she has noted so far. Driscoll passes their table, waves the air in front of her nose, and reminds the pair to be sure to smell the substances in the water.

Returning to her table group with goggles affixed properly, Tiana listens as D.J. reads directions aloud: "Put the crushed malachite in a large cup and add the pepper and water." Clearly, the lesson format incorporates student preferences for active kinesthetic participation. Dominic and D.J. cover their eyes with their goggles. After stirring the contents of the cup, D.J. says, "Okay, the similarities and differences: one similarity between the pepper and malachite is that they both have rocks in 'em." He writes this in his notes. Dominic shakes the cylinders and muses, "They both have grains." Tiana asks the group, "You got that they look like rocks, right? They have specks."

In the background, Driscoll can be heard advising a group, offering hints as to how to complete the double-bubble map. "They both have things that are different," she says. "When you look at them with the magnifying glass, the similarities and differences that you see can be used in the double bubble."

At a table in the center of the room, Nicholas, Tanisha, and Latrea draw Venn diagrams. "All right, the grains both are round," says Tanisha. At the next table, DiJuan and Marquez, who have been watching their neighbors draw Venn diagrams, now turn back to their own lab reports and sketch Venn diagrams. At a nearby table, Driscoll leans over to be close to three partners. Probing for extended and substantive oral responses, she asks, "What's gonna happen? The malachite with the water and the pepper with the water. Don't do it yet. *I* don't know what will happen. What's it say?" Folding the lab report open and pointing to the directions, she asks, "What's it say here?" As Jelan murmurs the directions to Driscoll and the group, Carnell responds, "Predict! Predict! Predict!" As she prepares to leave the table, Driscoll places her hand atop Carnell's head and says, "Prediction. *Pre* means 'before'." James asks, "Ms. Driscoll, can we mix 'em all together?" Driscoll responds, "Well, if we mix 'em all together, would we be able to answer the question, 'Do different things mix the same in water?'"

When the experiments are over, Driscoll brings the class together as a whole group to debrief the lesson. She calls on students to take turns adding traits to the double-bubble and T-chart graphic organizers on the board. The lesson ends with the class working as a group to answer the essential question of the lesson: How do different substances behave differently in water, and what are the implications for waste and drinking water? As in their small groups, students take on the challenge of completing a rigorous task, helping each other through reciprocal teaching, and demonstrating that knowledge creation and power are shared and developed together.

Walkthrough Wrap-Up

Before convening in the teachers' workroom for a facilitated feedback session, the walkthrough team gathers in the hallway outside Driscoll's classroom, taking a few minutes to make checks next to strategies that team members observed on their individual feedback forms and to add to the notes they made. Then, the observers each share the notes that they wrote at the bottom of their forms, in the section titled "What Teachers/Students Say/Do Related to the Focus Area." Here's what the teachers found:

Teacher 1

Teacher 1 observed that Driscoll ensured that each table group included boys and girls as well as students of varied ability levels. This teacher also noted that the students appeared to have learned their individual roles and responsibilities: When the "getters" were told to pick up their eye droppers, magnifying glasses, plastic cups of water, goggles, and plastic trays, they quickly did so and returned the equipment to their groups. Teacher 1 also noted that Driscoll circulated around the room, ensuring that groups had the tools and directions necessary to develop their expertise during small-group work.

Teacher 2

Teacher 2 saw that the routines and procedures that Driscoll had put in place to promote a collaborative approach toward learning supported the expectation that students would help each other in task completion. He felt that Driscoll clearly had developed her lesson format based on her students' preference for working in cohesive groups. Teacher 2 also observed that Driscoll balanced teacher-centered presentations to the whole class with guiding and facilitating student learning in small groups, that the groups used a variety of oral and written communication patterns, and that students treated each other with civility and respect (for example, by helping Tiana to properly affix her goggles).

Teacher 3

Teacher 3 noted that Driscoll helped Rani, James, Dyonnie, and other students understand their individual roles in content mastery and task completion by asking probing questions. She also observed that small groups such as Dominic and Tiana's used a variety of techniques to examine and record the traits they discovered during their experiments. Teacher 3 also noted that, from time to time, Driscoll reminded the whole class to use the Venn diagram as a graphic organizer ("Everybody in the group needs to make that double-bubble map of similarities and differences.").

Teacher 4

Teacher 4 noted that while students were conducting the experiments, Driscoll followed up on her opening directions by engaging in individual conversations with each of the nine table groups. Smiling at all times, she would stop her circuit of the room to make sure that groups focused on the appropriate

lab reports and used the flow map to help them remember the order of the procedures in the experiments.

Teacher 5

Teacher 5 noted the continuous level of interest and concern about the lesson that Driscoll and her students displayed. Starting at the beginning of the lesson, students carried out their reciprocal teaching roles, monitored and followed through on expectations by reading directions, picked up supplies when asked, and checked the progress of their work.

Teacher 5 also observed that the lesson ended with the class working as a group to develop understanding about the essential question of the lesson: How do different substances behave differently in water, and what are the implications for waste and drinking water? He saw Driscoll call on students, who then took turns adding traits to the graphic organizers on the board. Teacher 5 found that, both in their small-group and whole-class work, students took on the challenge of completing a rigorous task, assisting each other in learning by assuming the reciprocal roles of teacher and expert, and showing that they held important roles and information to help each other learn together.

10

Procedures for Rehearsal, Processing, and Transfer of Learning

In this chapter, we will examine how the PTP educators implemented the following strategies:

Category: Presenting Information and Ideas
Strategies: Teachers . . .
- Use a variety of modes of representing information and ideas.
- Use global (big-picture) as well as analytical (step-by-step) organizers to describe tasks, including
  - Graphic organizers and advance organizers;
  - Overviews, lesson outlines, and summarization guides;
  - Mnemonics and semantic mapping; and
  - Examples and analogies to concretize abstract ideas.

Category: Scaffolding between Prior Knowledge and New Learning
Strategies: Teachers . . .
- Provide modeling and cognitive scaffolding between prior knowledge and new learning.
- Connect new learning to students' prior knowledge using
  - Cultural metaphors,
  - Personal and relevant examples,
  - Multiple concrete representations, and
  - Explanations and models.

Category: Processing New Content

Strategies: Teachers . . .

- Help students process and internalize information presented.
- Create tools to help students understand information from readings, multimedia resources, site visits, and guests.
- Provide modeling and guided practice prior to student demonstrations and tests.
- Use procedures for elaboration of new concepts.
- Use culturally responsive strategies such as call and response, inside-outside discussion circle, visual imagery, and storytelling.
- Use accelerated learning techniques with students at all ability and performance levels, including
    - Rehearsal,
    - Repetition and periodic review,
    - Chunking,
    - Music as a memory aid, and
    - Memory association maps.

Category: Maintaining Active Participation and Managing Time Allocations

Strategies: Teachers . . .

- Engage students in multiple ways.
- Call on every student regularly.
- Frequently call for extended, substantive oral and written student responses.
- Maintain active learning by using questions and recitation and encouraging student-developed questions.
- Maintain active participation by randomly calling on students.
- Maintain kinesthetic participation.

- Actively engage students in tasks a great deal of the time.
- Allow students extended learning time as needed.

Category: Ensuring Rigor and Appropriate Task Difficulty

Strategies: Teachers . . .

- Continually and appropriately challenge students.
- Regularly remind students that learning will be challenging and rigorous.
- Use challenging materials and tasks.
- Create productive learning environments.
- Use current learning materials and technology.

Presenting Information and Ideas

According to Shade, Kelly, and Oberg (1997), effective and culturally responsive teachers explicitly teach their students the processes involved in knowledge construction and higher-level thinking skills such as metacognition. In addition, Irvine and Armento (2001) suggest that to help students understand information and transfer knowledge from readings, multimedia resources, site visits and guests, effective teachers use tools such as graphic and advance organizers, mnemonics and semantic mapping, lesson overviews, outlines, and summarization guides.

Almost all the PTP principals recounted how the teachers at their schools used a variety of graphic organizers and other techniques to help students process and transfer information learned in their classrooms, particularly those they learned from the National Urban Alliance (NUA) Literacy Initiative. For instance, middle school principal Bridget Lawley noted that teacher Lisa Forsythe used such strategies "to help students organize their thinking, analyze literature, and map ideas from reading and prior to writing." According to Adrianne Driscoll, such strategies "help students to compartmentalize in their minds and create associations and deep understandings of terms and concepts that they can go back to and retrieve later." She noted that the NUA strategies "basically work fairly well with everybody," but especially well for "scholars who lack some of the background knowledge expected at their grade level." Driscoll also noted that the NUA strategies met her students' motivational needs as they worked to meet grade-level expectations. "The NUA strategies give them something to start with, which is really important for our kids," she said. "Consequently, a lot of them say, 'Now I'm understanding; I'm getting *A*s, and before I was failing.' They like the strategies that we use."

Sixth grade teacher Danielle Kaplan said that she strongly believes in note-taking as a study strategy to help middle-level students develop higher-level metacognitive skills. "Note-taking is a big skill," she said. "All year, students take notes about directions, work processes, project steps, and then about content." For her students, note-taking served a function similar to that of graphic organizers: helping students draw out important information worthy of retention and "organize their thoughts."

Lisa Forsythe noted that she liked to combine the accelerated learning strategy of repetition with that of providing global and analytical plans for assignments and projects. She believed that "repeating back is a way of refocusing kids and asking: 'Are you tuning in?'" She often stated guidelines that were written on the board or a project sheet so that students understood their individual roles in task mastery. For each step, she would have students repeat back to her, asking, "What is the first thing you need to do?" "What's the second thing?" She said that after several repetitions, the students would start to criticize her. "That's where the kids say, 'Okay, we get it!'" she said. "But I do feel that it has improved the quality of work in my classroom as well as understanding of success expectations. In the end, they appreciate my giving them clear guidelines."

Processing New Content

In their verbal interactions to help their students process new content, PTP teachers drew on such strategies as call and response, inside-outside discussion circle, visual imagery, and storytelling. Middle school teacher Susan Lansing found that students "become very excited" and are motivated by their "visualization of three-dimensional objects." Chloe Gifford also found her students were motivated when she incorporated opportunities for them to share stories during lessons. "Black people are storytelling people," she said. "My students like sharing their own stories."

According to Cole (1995), techniques such as rehearsal, repetition and periodic review, chunking, using music as a memory aid, memory association maps, and guided practice have been shown to help students accelerate learning. Principal Alicia Baldwin saw Chloe Gifford not only teaching students to self-assess work samples, but also providing them with multiple opportunities to make corrections. Elementary school principal Joanne Stewart observed 3rd grade teacher Mark Goldberg using practice, recitation, and call and response to help students remember the school pledge, the names of the continents and oceans, and literary pieces for school assemblies, among other things. "The kids love choral recitation—performing readers' theatre scripts where they *become* the parts," he said. Noting the relation of call and response to black culture and heritage, Adrianne Driscoll said that it was "really an excellent strategy for black kids. I've had kids come in here not knowing any multiplication, and after doing call and response for the first half of the school year, they can all multiply up to 12 times 12. We then add higher concepts, such as squaring and cubing numbers, and they get that as well. This strategy works really well with our kids."

Using Current Materials and Technology

PTP classrooms were physically inviting and richly appointed with current learning materials and technology that helped teachers attend to multiple concurrent student needs and allow learning through multiple channels. Teacher Danielle Kaplan went so far as to post PowerPoint presentations containing assignment steps on her own webpage. Jeffrey Brooks used microphones and PowerPoint presentations to help students see, hear, and read content, and also made use of a multimedia instruction station, infusing his lessons with content from the Internet and integrating interactive games for reading and mathematics into instruction. Principal Sela Hadžić attributed Charles Ackerman's success with students to daily use of the school computer lab. David Lee even used film-editing software to record videos providing students with feedback.

As principal Darrell Conway noted, "technology is so much a part of kids' lives right now, it would be foolish not to use that as an instructional strategy. Closing the achievement gap will depend upon all our children being able to access and use technology in a very critical and creative manner."

A Virtual Walk through Adrianne Driscoll's 6th Grade Math Lesson

As two teams of three teachers apiece enter Adrianne Driscoll's classroom, they note that she has arranged supplies for her mathematics lesson on a table. On the wall, among posters of African and African American personages, vocabulary terms, and pictures of students, Driscoll has added posters showing the graphic organizers that will be used in today's lesson. Her students, all of whom are black, sit in table groups of four facing the whiteboard. Driscoll has varied the group composition at each table to include low- and middle-ability students alongside high-ability students, students who are familiar with the tasks alongside a few who have been absent for the past few days, and males and females.

The goal of the day's lesson is written on the whiteboard: "Scholars will learn the properties of quadrilaterals." As the students take their seats, Driscoll requests that they quiet down for the reading of the directions. The students quickly heed her request. "Today we will be *building quadrilaterals*," Driscoll says, emphasizing the last two words. She has the students repeat the word "quadrilaterals" several times in choral response. Then, she calls for a reader to begin reading the top of a specified page in the math textbook while the rest of the class reads along. Many students wave their hands to be called on, and Driscoll lets them know that she will call on a second reader later. She selects Sasha and thanks her for volunteering. As Sasha reads, Driscoll walks around the room. She touches Marquez on the shoulder as she passes him, opens the book to the correct page for Jelan at the back of the room, answers a request for a pencil from April in the center of room, then returns to the front of the room to review the directions. She enthuses about the prospect of building a Venn diagram, or "double bubble": "Ooh, I hear a double bubble! Ooh! Now I need someone to read the problem. Exactly what are we going to be doing?"

Smiling at Terrell, who is holding his hand up to read, Driscoll asks playfully, "Didn't you read for me yesterday?" Nicholas wonders aloud if the class will get points added to a Skate Party tally sheet. "Yes, you'll get points if you are quietly listening," responds Driscoll. She chooses DiJuan to read the directions for the math investigation, which entails determining whether it's possible to create quadrilaterals given sides of specified lengths.

Tiana and Carnell take on the responsibility of passing out brads and strips of paper, while DJ and Shakir hand out one instruction book to each group for the investigation. In addition, each student retrieves a die from the supplies table. Terrell asks Driscoll how they will determine the length of the sides of the shapes. She gets everyone's attention and announces that each student is to roll his or her die three times, and the third number that he or she comes up with will be the length of one of the sides.

The students get to work. In one group, Mikela takes on the important role of coaching Neveah: "Okay, 11, 14, and 6, and 6. We gotta connect that." Neveah asks why they have two sixes, and Mikela explains that Marquez rolled one of them. She continues in her reciprocal teaching role, explaining to Neveah how to measure the length of the sides and how the shapes are to be made: "Oh you don't know how to connect 'em 'cause you weren't here yesterday. The first hole in the strip of paper is zero, don't count that one. Then, you count the next one. You go: zero, one, two, three, four five, six."

The two girls share brads and strips and center the instruction book between them so that both can see the directions. As Mikela shows Neveah how to connect the end of one strip to the other using a brad, Neveah asks, "We stop at fourteen?" Mikela responds, "Remember, don't count the first one." Together, they count the holes representing the lengths of the sides and insert the brads. "This is *way* fun, Ms. Driscoll!" announces Marquez.

Using mathematical language, Driscoll maintains the rigor of the learning task by reminding students to be sure to insert the brads at the *vertex*. Across the room, she confirms to a group of students that they appear to have made a quadrilateral and asks them to trace it on their paper. "That's a cool quadrilateral," she tells another group. "It's got four sides!"

Back at the front of the room, Driscoll confers with Gerald, who has made an irregular quadrilateral, and lets him know that she doesn't agree with him that it is a parallelogram. The two of them bend his shape at the vertices held by brads until the sides are almost parallel. "Now it's really close," says Driscoll. Gerald takes the shape back to his group.

All around the room, students are helping each other make four-sided shapes, closely scrutinizing and bending the shapes they've made and tracing the shapes onto paper. At a table in the center of the room, Tyree smiles at his partner as he makes an X-shape using his four sides, disassembles it, and then forms a rhombus-like shape. At another table, Driscoll helps Simi through each step of forming the shape, then coaches her repeatedly, assuring her that she can pronounce "quadrilateral" after having made the shape. For students who are more capable, such as those at Sephora's table, Driscoll's role is to confirm their new discoveries and applaud their attempts at connecting their sides in more than one way.

Drawing the class back together as a whole group, Driscoll congratulates the students for creating "both strange and beautiful" quadrilaterals, which gets a laugh from the students. Reinforcing the students' collective efforts and positive behavior, she adds points to the class's Skating Party tally sheet. Then, to highlight the variety of solutions at which students might have arrived, Driscoll urges students to observe each others' work, asking a few of them to stand and show their drawings. As the students report the differences they observed using sides of similar or different lengths, Driscoll records the various lengths of the sides in a chart on the board next to the word "Data."

To help students consider the evolution of their conclusions and think about the ideas they have developed, Driscoll brings Malika's shape to the attention of the entire class, pointing out that when Malika made it, she didn't know that it was a quadrilateral. Honoring Malika's work and asking her to model and share her thinking with the class, Driscoll asks why she didn't think the shape was a quadrilateral, and what made her change her mind. Malika traces the shape with her finger, pointing out that it looks somewhat like a triangle even though it has four sides.

The students continue to share their thinking about the kinds of shapes that they've made. Although Driscoll writes the responses on the board for all the class to view, she reminds students to write their responses on their own, in complete sentences. Scaffolding the kinds of responses required on the state performance assessment, she points out that were this assignment on the WASL, the students would want to write in complete sentences and refer to their drawn examples by writing "See examples below."

The class erupts with groans and half-hearted protests when Driscoll announces that they will now transition to creating a "double-bubble" map to summarize properties of quadrilaterals and nonquadrilaterals. She resists the groans, knowing full well that when students deeply understand subject matter, they can identify examples and non-examples of various concepts. She tells the students that she will choose among those who are finished writing, raise their hands, have their feet on the floor, and are sitting quietly to select the color of the marker that the class will use to complete the graphic organizer. As she hangs the easel paper on which to draw the Venn diagram, Driscoll interrupts herself to ask the class to pick a Disney character from the cards hanging along the edge of the board. Often, she will take a moment to play a game in which the students guess which Disney character is on her socks. After the students select Winnie the Pooh, Driscoll lifts her pant leg to reveal that the students guessed correctly, and everyone laughs.

Returning to the group task, Driscoll calls on students to take turns adding traits to the Venn diagram on the easel paper after labeling one of the circles "triangle" and the other "quadrilaterals." Prompting the class in tone of a game-show host ("And now we go to . . . Kimaru!"), she asks the class what triangles and quadrilaterals have in common. "They're all shapes," says Tyra. Dominque adds that "they are polygons," to which Driscoll replies, "Many-sided figures." Reminding students that "raising your hand is a wonderful thing," Driscoll asks Ronisha for a trait. She responds that both shapes have corners. Driscoll asks the class what the mathematical term for corners is; they shout in unison, "Vertices!"

Next, Driscoll says that they will now list differences between triangles and quadrilaterals.

She calls on Harsha, who quickly responds, "Triangles have three sides, and quadrilaterals have four sides." Then she calls on Chris, who requires some prompting to help him remember traits of triangles. Driscoll gives him a hint by waving a shape around, and finally he recalls that triangles have three vertices, and quadrilaterals have four.

Walkthrough Wrap-Up

Before convening in the teachers' workroom for a facilitated feedback session, the walkthrough team gathers in the hallway outside Driscoll's classroom, taking a few minutes to make checks next to strategies that team members observed on their individual feedback forms and to add to the notes they made. Then, the observers each share the notes that they wrote at the bottom of their forms, in the section titled "What Teachers/Students Say/Do Related to the Focus Area." Here's what the teachers found:

Teacher 1

Teacher 1 observed that Driscoll supported the development of students' self-efficacy by urging them to observe each others' work and having them voice diverse perspectives on their discoveries. This teacher was particularly impressed by the positive feedback Driscoll offered to Malika when she asked her why she didn't originally think her shape was a quadrilateral and what made her change her mind. Teacher 1 also noted that Driscoll reinforced the students' efforts by congratulating them on their "strange and beautiful" shapes and adding points to the Skating Party tally sheet.

Teacher 2

Teacher 2 thought that Driscoll displayed "withitness" by using multiple strategies to attend to students' needs throughout the lesson. She made sure that students had access to necessary resources (by providing a pencil for April, for example, and opening a book to the correct page for Jelan) and showed caring by thanking Sasha for reading the lesson's instructions. Teacher 2 also observed that Driscoll provided the modeling and support that Gerald needed to build a quadrilateral by pointing out that his shape was "really close" to being a parallelogram.

Teacher 3

Teacher 3 noted that the social interactions in Driscoll's class were overwhelmingly positive. He pointed out how Driscoll touched Marquez on the shoulder in a caring way as she passed him while circulating the room, and how she playfully asked Terrell, "Didn't you read for me yesterday?"

Teacher 4

Teacher 4 observed that Driscoll promoted student interest in what they were learning by enthusing about the prospect of building a Venn diagram ("Ooh, I hear a double-bubble map! How are they the same? How are they different?"). The teacher also noted that Driscoll's frequent references to the purpose and goal of the day's activities helped ensure students' success by helping them understand the expected outcomes.

Teacher 5

Teacher 5 noted that Driscoll had put structures in place to support small-group work where students develop their expertise by ensuring that group compositions were varied. The teacher also observed that Mikela took on a reciprocal teaching role in her group, explaining to Neveah how to measure the length of sides and put the shapes together. She also found that students' movements showed that they had learned their roles and responsibilities in completing tasks, such as when Tiana and Carnell passed out supplies to the groups. Additionally, Teacher 5 observed that Driscoll clearly had chosen the lesson format based on her students' preferences for working in cohesive groups. The teacher also observed that Driscoll set the expectation that students would assume individual roles in content mastery and task completion, reminding them to write their responses out in complete sentences.

Teacher 6

Teacher 6 noted that Driscoll had students repeat the word "quadrilaterals" several times in choral response to her slow pronunciation of the world. The teacher also observed that Driscoll called upon students to add traits to the Venn diagram on the white board, using the gestures and inflections of a game show host to help make the routine activity exciting. Teacher 6 noted that by writing and reading aloud student responses, Driscoll helped students to derive and convey meaning from written text and speech.

Afterword

Fundamental to democratic principles of education is the expectation of ensuring the highest possible educational attainment for every learner. Appropriate pedagogical responses for all learners draw on comparing current practices to research-based policies and practices, collecting data on the effectiveness of current practices, and strategically developing new practices and strategies to meet students' needs.

Researchers have suggested that there are patterns of effective and culturally responsive strategies that can be discerned by examining the practices of educators like those discussed in this book. The interrelated strategies used in PTP classrooms are consistent with considerable research on the teacher behaviors that most influence learning and maximize student learning by responding to diverse students' traits. While there is much we can learn from the exemplary PTP teachers, it is important to recall that they are not unlike their fellow educators throughout the United States. They helped their students to close the achievement gap by recognizing and nurturing linked self-efficacy beliefs; attention to the social context for learning; and professional development, reflection, collaboration, and coaching to enhance their instructional capabilities. My hope is that the strategies I've presented in this book will help teachers to strengthen their professional practice and increase black students' achievement.

Assessment of Effective and Culturally Responsive Strategies (AECRS) Form

Assessment of Effective and Culturally Responsive Strategies (AECRS) Form

HOW TO USE THIS FORM: Staff members first select one or more of the categories below based on perceived needs and areas of interest within their school. Educators then individually rate the frequency of use of each strategy within the category or categories on a scale of 1 (lowest frequency) to 10 (highest frequency). Teams or work groups then come together to calculate a group average for the frequency of use for each strategy. Individuals and groups may use analyses of these data along with common interests to identify categories on which to concentrate their attention as they develop and try out strategies.

Category 1: Setting and Maintaining Clear Expectations for Content Mastery		
Frequency (1–10)	**1A: Belief in Self-Efficacy**	**Notes**
	Believing in the capacity to make a difference in student learning	
	Strengthening skills, knowledge, and self-efficacy through professional learning	
Frequency (1–10)	**1B: Role and Mastery Expectations**	**Notes**
	Holding high academic and personal expectations for every child	
	Holding students to established state and district standards	
	Setting objectives and providing regular feedback on accomplishment	
	Regularly reminding students that they are expected to learn	
	Ensuring that students understand their individual roles in content mastery and task completion	
Frequency (1–10)	**1C: Equitable Access to Resources and Opportunities to Learn**	**Notes**
	Providing students with equitable access to learning opportunities regardless of academic gaps or needs	
	Providing resources to meet the needs of all children regardless of academic gaps or needs	
Frequency (1–10)	**1D: Fostering Student Self-Efficacy and Responsibility**	**Notes**
	Believing in and promoting student self-efficacy, individual ability to achieve, and positive self-regard	
	Scaffolding and gradually transferring learning responsibility to students, teaching them to self-monitor skills development	
	Providing developmentally appropriate choices and decisions about alternative assignments to reach academic goals	
	Fostering students' abilities to persevere on learning tasks	
	Regularly reminding students that learning will be challenging and rigorous	
	Providing instruction and extensive modeling on how to strategize in the face of difficulty	
	Reinforcing student effort and recognizing accomplishments	

	Category 2: Student-Teacher Social Interactions	
Frequency (1–10)	**2A: Caring**	Notes
	Creating inviting environments that reflect personal caring	
	Developing positive, personal relationships with students	
	Encouraging a sense of family and community	
	Stressing collectiveness and collaboration, rather than individuality, in interactions	
	Listening to and encouraging mutual sharing of personal experiences related to curriculum	
	Providing mentoring and emotional support	
	Extending relationships with and caring for students beyond the classroom	
Frequency (1–10)	**2B: Fairness and Respect**	Notes
	Basing interactions on human dignity principles, respect for every person, and an attitude of hope and optimism	
	Creating situations for all students to succeed	
	Promoting student interactions based on principles of democracy, equity, and justice	
Frequency (1–10)	**2C: Low Favoritism**	Notes
	Treating all students equally well	
	Providing each student with equitable access to learning resources and opportunities to learn.	
Frequency (1–10)	**2D: Low Friction**	Notes
	Ensuring that students and teachers treat each other with civility, gentleness, and support	
	Handling disagreements with discussion and respect for alternative positions	

	Category 3: Classroom Climate	
Frequency (1–10)	**3A: Cohesiveness**	Notes
	Promoting a group-centered, collaborative approach to learning	
	Promoting a positive, familial classroom climate	
	Grouping students according to shared traits to stimulate enjoyment and cohesiveness	
	Identifying and counteracting stereotypes by teaching students about universal traits and values	

	Understanding that classroom instruction reflects elements of both the community and school	
	Involving family and community in student's learning	
	Creating positive relationships and collaborating meaningfully with parents and community members to further the educational development of students	
Frequency (1–10)	**3B: Low Apathy**	**Notes**
	Fostering both student and teacher interest in teaching and learning	
	Arousing student curiosity and explaining the purpose and practical application of content	
	Promoting student interest in what goes on in class	
Frequency (1–10)	**3C: Productive Learning Environments**	**Notes**
	Maintaining a safe and orderly classroom	
	Balancing established routines and rituals with excitement	
	Establishing a physically inviting classroom	
	Understanding that the classroom climate reflects elements of both the community and school	

Category 4: Classroom Management		
Frequency (1–10)		**Notes**
	Using appropriate language	
	Disciplining using an adult voice	
	Tempering order and established standards with equal parts respect—being caring, yet firm	
	Preventing situations where students lose peer respect	
	Responding to misbehavior on an individual basis	
	Matching discipline to students' home culture and language	
	Providing explicit coaching on appropriate behavior	
	Explicitly communicating expectations of students' roles and behaviors	
	Teaching mediation and coping skills	

Category 5: Curriculum and Instructional Design		
Frequency (1–10)	**5A: Alignment of Goals, Standards, Instruction, and Assessment**	**Notes**
	Developing clear goals and standards	
	Designing instruction aligned to curriculum content and authentic assessment methods	
	Aligning assessments to the content, format, and complexity or level of difficulty of teaching and learning activities	
Frequency (1–10)	**5B: Careful Instructional Planning**	**Notes**
	Carefully planning and clearly structuring day and lesson content	
	Structuring lessons to include review of mastered material	
	Using varied systematic strategies for direct reading instruction, such as using encoding principles and maintaining an upbeat climate	
Frequency (1–10)	**5C: Planning for Student Engagement**	**Notes**
	Carefully planning the day and lessons to include active engagement	
	Designing structured classes and daily routines	
	Having and stating specific and explicit activity objectives	
	Balancing facilitation of student learning with teacher-centered presentations to the whole class	
	Helping arouse student curiosity by helping students understand the purpose of learning content	
Frequency (1–10)	**5D: Personalized Instruction**	**Notes**
	Planning activities to meet the individual developmental needs of diverse students	
	Allowing students to share in lesson planning	
Frequency (1–10)	**5E: Planning for Cooperative Group Instruction**	**Notes**
	Structuring environments for cooperative learning and group activities	
	Structuring group tasks to ensure that students share important roles and develop expertise	
	Structuring group composition to balance familiar and unfamiliar group members	
	Ensuring that group goals are attainable	

Category 6: Classroom-Based Assessment		
Frequency (1–10)		**Notes**
	Aligning instruction and curriculum content to authentic assessment methods	
	Aligning assessments to the content, format, and complexity or level of difficulty of teaching and learning activities	
	Using frequent continuous assessments to determine skills and knowledge, provide feedback on goals attainment, and create interventions	
	Augmenting standardized tests with a variety of assessment strategies appropriate to diverse learners, including observations, oral examinations, and performances	
	Making decisions using multiple samples of students' best efforts toward meeting standards, consistently scored against public criteria	
	Teaching students how to self-assess and monitor development of skills, knowledge, and dispositions	
	Using culturally sensitive, fair, and unbiased assessments of cognitive and social skills	
	Matching assessment to students' language and home culture	
	Ensuring that language abilities and special needs do not interfere with demonstration of competence by providing coaching, accommodations, and translation support as needed	
	Varying content, time, and format of assessment sessions in response to students' energy levels and engagement patterns	

Category 7: Cultural Competence		
Frequency (1–10)	**7A: Cultural Understanding and Awareness**	**Notes**
	Understanding how race, ethnicity, language, socioeconomic status, gender, history, residential status, and cultural experience influence behavior, performance, and climate	
	Demonstrating knowledge of the modal beliefs, personalities, and interaction, communication, and linguistic styles of varied cultural groups	
	Understanding cultural variations and nuances of communication related to verbal and nonverbal cues such as gestures, timing, walking, eye glances, dress, and presentation style	
	Demonstrating knowledge of the diversity of cultural, ethnic, linguistic, and gender groups in the classroom	
	Demonstrating knowledge of students' backgrounds	
	Understanding the effect of cultural experience on how students construct knowledge	

	Understanding the effect of racism on students	
	Understanding aspects of one's own culture that facilitate or hinder communication with one's own and other cultural groups	
Frequency (1–10)	**7B: Sensitivity to and Valuing of Cultural Difference**	**Notes**
	Communicating validation and acceptance of cultural and gender differences to students	
	Showing genuine respect for cultural pride and diversity	
	Fostering students' ability to function in their culture of origin	
Frequency (1–10)	**7C: Information in Curriculum on Cultural Differences**	**Notes**
	Using curriculum materials that describe historical, social, and political events from a wide range of racial, ethnic, cultural, and language perspectives	
	Investigating topics related to ethnicity, gender, and exceptionality from a wide range of racial, ethnic, cultural, and language perspectives	
	Helping each student understand his or her personal perspective, or "self," as one of many cultural perspectives	
	Providing curriculum materials on social, economic, and political issues related to ethnicity, gender, and exceptionality	
	Helping students understand how personal and cultural experiences influence how they and others construct knowledge	
	Providing factual information to refute misconceptions and prejudices about ethnic group members	
	Understanding and using information about students' families, cultures, and communities to connect to learning activities	
	Encouraging mutual sharing of personal and expressive stories related to content	
Frequency (1–10)	**7D: Cultural Critique and Activism**	**Notes**
	Helping students understand, critique, and change social structures and practices that produce inequities	
	Providing opportunities for students to critique concepts learned, their origins, and their authors' economic, political, and social perspectives and motivations	
	Being involved in political struggles aimed at achieving a more just and humane society	
	Urging collective action grounded in cultural understanding, experiences, and ways of knowing the world	
	Helping students learn how to change elements of society held up to critique	
	Providing students with experiences making decisions and taking action about real-world problems	

Category 8: Cultural Congruence in Instruction		
Frequency (1-10)	**8A: Meaningful, Complex Instruction**	**Notes**
	Using constructivist approaches with student knowledge as the basis for inquiry, representing ideas, developing meaning, elaborating, organizing, and interacting with content	
	Teaching a continuum of basic to higher-order literacy skills, knowledge, and ways of thinking to help students derive and convey meaning from text and speech, solve problems, achieve goals, develop individual knowledge and potential, and participate in society	
	Developing metacognitive skills that help children learn how to learn	
	Providing large amounts of time reading a great variety of texts	
	Engaging in collaborative team teaching	
	Engaging all students using meaningful, relevant, and challenging curriculum, content, and instructional activities	
	Teaching concepts and skills using integrated, holistic, interdisciplinary lessons	
	Engaging students in real-life, project-based contextual and vocational activities	
	Teaching skills within the context of meaningful applications	
Frequency (1-10)	**8B: Scaffolding Instruction to Home Culture and Language**	**Notes**
	Teaching to historical, cultural, social, ethnic, and linguistic differences	
	Providing scaffolding to match or link curriculum, materials, lesson content and format, and instructional methods to students' home culture, interests, experiences, and prior learning	
	Scaffolding and engaging students' learning using visual images and familiar vocabulary to connect prior knowledge and new learning	
	Providing core instruction in Standard English	
	Teaching academic content in preschool	
Frequency (1-10)	**8C: Responding to Student Traits and Needs**	**Notes**
	Demonstrating knowledge of content	
	Understanding and using speech and expressions familiar to students	
	Selecting and using a variety of instructional methods and interactive strategies	
	Varying strategies to meet student's motivational preferences	
	Matching instructional strategies to student traits, abilities, and learning style preferences	

	Promoting student use of multiple intelligences to gain, use, and respond to knowledge	
	Providing materials and learning centers for varied styles and modalities	
	Allowing students to express visual, tactile, emotional, and auditory preferences	
	Incorporating student preferences for verbal expressiveness	
	Incorporating student preferences for active kinesthetic participation	
	Limiting lectures to 5–10 minutes and augment with visuals and examples	
Frequency (1-10)	**8D: Culturally Relevant Curriculum and Materials**	**Notes**
	Selecting and using culturally relevant curriculum materials from and containing all cultural groups	
	Selecting and using culturally relevant visual representations of all cultural groups	
	Selecting and use culturally relevant books, pictures, and bulletin board items	
	Recognizing culturally relevant events	
	Using manipulatives, models, artifacts, and concrete representations of concepts	
	Using primary (original) source materials	

Category 9: Cooperative Group Instruction		
Frequency (1–10)	**9A: Group Environment and Composition**	**Notes**
	Structuring environments to allow for cooperative learning and group activities	
	Creating flexible student groupings	
	Balancing familiar and unfamiliar group members when structuring groups	
	Creating low-high mixed dyads to enhance achievement for students	
	Regularly placing students in groups mixed by race, gender, and ability	
	Balancing facilitated student learning with teacher-centered whole-class presentations	
Frequency (1–10)	**9B: Student Collaboration and Efficacy Development**	**Notes**
	Promoting a group-centered collaborative approach toward learning	
	Honoring students' preference for cohesive group participation when formatting lessons	

	Promoting student-to-student assistance for most learning tasks	
	Using a variety of oral and written communication patterns, including pair, team, and whole-class responses following collaborative work	
	Ensuring that tasks are doable and group goals are attainable	
	Ensuring that students understand individual roles in content mastery and task completion	
	Ensuring that all students in groups share important roles and demonstrate their expertise during small-group tasks	
	Scaffolding learning and gradually transferring responsibility to students, teaching students to self-monitor skills and knowledge development	
	Providing scaffolding through reciprocal teaching in which students gradually assume the role of teacher, helping their peers with learning tasks	
	Providing instruction and practice in comprehension strategies such as predicting, generating questions, clarifying, and summarizing using authentic texts	

Category 10: Procedures for Rehearsal, Processing, and Transfer of Learning		
Frequency (1–10)	**10A: Presenting Information and Ideas**	**Notes**
	Using a variety of modes of representing information and ideas	
	Using global (big-picture) as well as analytical (step-by-step) organizers to describe tasks, including graphic organizers and advance organizers; overviews, lesson outlines, and summarization guides; mnemonics and semantic mapping; and examples and analogies to concretize abstract ideas.	
Frequency (1–10)	**10B: Scaffolding between Prior Knowledge and New Learning**	**Notes**
	Providing modeling and cognitive scaffolding between prior knowledge and new learning	
	Connecting new learning to students' prior knowledge using cultural metaphors, personal and relevant examples, multiple concrete representations, and explanations and models	
Frequency (1–10)	**10C: Processing New Content**	**Notes**
	Helping students process and internalize information presented	
	Creating tools to help students understand information from readings, multimedia resources, site visits, and guests	
	Providing modeling and guided practice prior to student demonstrations and tests	
	Using procedures for elaboration of new concepts	
	Using culturally responsive strategies such as call and response, inside-outside discussion circle, visual imagery, and storytelling	

Frequency (1–10)		Notes
	Using accelerated learning techniques with students at all ability and performance levels, including rehearsal, repetition and periodic review, chunking, music as a memory aid, and memory association maps	
Frequency (1–10)	**10D: Maintaining Active Participation and Managing Time Allocations**	**Notes**
	Engaging students in multiple ways	
	Calling on every student regularly	
	Frequently calling for extended, substantive oral and written student responses	
	Maintaining active learning by using questions and recitation and encouraging student-developed questions	
	Maintaining active participation by randomly calling on students	
	Maintaining kinesthetic participation	
	Actively engaging students in tasks a great deal of the time	
	Allowing students extended learning time as needed	
Frequency (1–10)	**10E: Ensuring Rigor and Appropriate Task Difficulty**	**Notes**
	Continually and appropriately challenging students	
	Regularly reminding students that learning will be challenging and rigorous	
	Using challenging materials and tasks	
	Creating productive learning environments	
	Using current learning materials and technology	

Appendix B

Walkthrough Feedback Forms

Note: To access these forms online,
go to http://www.ascd.org/publications/books/110004.aspx
and follow the link for Appendix B.
The password for downloading the forms is 110004.

WALKTHROUGH FEEDBACK FORM #1:
Setting and Maintaining Clear Expectations for Content Mastery

Date: _____   Teacher: _____

Grade Level: _____   Subject: _____

Category: 1A (Belief in Self-Efficacy)

Evidence observed that the teacher . . .

Believes in his or her capacity to make a difference in student learning:

_____

_____

_____

_____

Strengthens skills, knowledge, and self-efficacy through professional learning:

_____

_____

_____

_____

Evidence expected, but not seen:

_____

_____

_____

_____

Category: 1B (Role and Mastery Expectations)

Evidence observed that the teacher . . .

Holds high academic and personal expectations for every child:

_____

_____

_____

_____

Holds students to established state and district standards:

_____

_____

_____

_____

Sets objectives and provides regular feedback on accomplishment:

_____

_____

_____

_____

Regularly reminds students that they are expected to learn:

_____

_____

_____

_____

Ensures that students understand their individual roles in content mastery and task completion:

_____

_____

_____

_____

Evidence expected, but not seen:

_____

_____

_____

_____

Category: 1C (Equitable Access to Resources and Opportunities to Learn)

Evidence observed that the teacher . . .

Provides students with equitable access to learning opportunities regardless of academic gaps or needs:

_____

_____

_____

_____

Provides resources to meet the needs of all children regardless of academic gaps or needs:

_____

_____

_____

_____

Evidence expected, but not seen:

_____

_____

_____

_____

Category: 1D (Fostering Student Self-Efficacy and Responsibility)

Evidence observed that the teacher . . .

Believes in and promotes student self-efficacy, individual ability to achieve, and positive self-regard:

_____

_____

_____

_____

Scaffolds and gradually transfers learning responsibility to students, teaching them to self-monitor skills development:

_____

_____

_____

_____

Provides developmentally appropriate choices and decisions about alternative assignments to reach academic goals:

_____

_____

_____

_____

Fosters students' abilities to persevere on learning tasks:

_____

_____

_____

_____

Regularly reminds students that learning will be challenging and rigorous:

_____

_____

_____

_____

Provides instruction and extensive modeling on how to strategize in the face of difficulty:

_____

_____

_____

_____

Reinforces student effort and recognizes accomplishments:

_____

_____

_____

_____

Evidence expected, but not seen:

_____

_____

_____

_____

Goals Moving Forward		
Strategy/Activity	**Expected Impact**	**Start & End Dates**
(*Example:* Teams will review learning style inventories and use results to implement research-based instructional strategies that address the learning style preferences of black students.) _____ _____ _____ _____ _____ _____ _____	(*Example:* December 2011 walkthrough data will show average increases in use of strategies that address the learning style preferences of black students from 29 percent to 59 percent.) _____ _____ _____ _____ _____ _____ _____	(*Example:* 5/31/11–12/16/11) _____ _____

WALKTHROUGH FEEDBACK FORM #2:
Student-Teacher Social Interactions

Date: _____   Teacher: _____

Grade Level: _____   Subject: _____

Category: 2A (Caring)

Evidence observed that the teacher . . .

Creates inviting environments that reflect personal caring:

_____

_____

_____

_____

Develops positive, personal relationships with students:

_____

_____

_____

_____

Encourages a sense of family and community:

_____

_____

_____

_____

Stresses collectiveness and collaboration, rather than individuality, in interactions:

_____

_____

_____

_____

Listens to and encourages mutual sharing of personal experiences related to curriculum:

_____

_____

_____

_____

Provides mentoring and emotional support:

_____

_____

_____

_____

Extends relationships with and caring for students beyond the classroom:

_____

_____

_____

_____

Evidence expected, but not seen:

_____

_____

_____

_____

Category: 2B (Fairness and Respect)

Evidence observed that the teacher . . .

Bases interactions on human dignity principles, respect for every person, and an attitude of hope and optimism:

_____

_____

_____

_____

Creates situations for all students to succeed:

_____

_____

_____

_____

Promotes student interactions based on principles of democracy, equity, and justice:

_____

_____

_____

_____

Evidence expected, but not seen:

_____

_____

_____

Category: 2C (Low Favoritism)

Evidence observed that the teacher . . .

Treats all students equally well:

_____

_____

_____

_____

Provides each student with equitable access to learning resources and opportunities to learn:

_____

_____

_____

_____

Evidence expected, but not seen:

_____

_____

_____

_____

Category: 2D (Low Friction)

Evidence observed that the teacher . . .

Ensures that students and teachers treat each other with civility, gentleness, and support:

_____

_____

_____

_____

Handles disagreements with discussion and respect for alternative positions:

_____

_____

_____

_____

Evidence expected, but not seen:

_____

_____

_____

_____

Goals Moving Forward		
Strategy/Activity	**Expected Impact**	**Start & End Dates**
(*Example:* Teams will review learning style inventories and use results to implement research-based instructional strategies that address the learning style preferences of black students.)	(*Example:* December 2011 walkthrough data will show average increases in use of strategies that address the learning style preferences of black students from 29 percent to 59 percent.)	(*Example:* 5/31/11–12/16/11)

WALKTHROUGH FEEDBACK FORM #3:
Classroom Climate

Date: _____   Teacher: _____

Grade Level: _____   Subject: _____

Category: 3A (Cohesiveness)

Evidence observed that the teacher . . .

Promotes a group-centered, collaborative approach to learning:

_____

_____

_____

_____

Promotes a positive, familial classroom climate:

_____

_____

_____

_____

Groups students according to shared traits to stimulate enjoyment and cohesiveness:

_____

_____

_____

_____

Identifies and counteracts stereotypes by teaching students about universal traits and values:

_____

_____

_____

_____

Understands that classroom instruction reflects elements of both the community and school:

_____

_____

_____

_____

Involves family and community in students' learning:

_____

_____

_____

_____

Creates positive relationships and collaborates meaningfully with parents and community members to further the educational development of students:

_____

_____

_____

_____

Evidence expected, but not seen:

_____

_____

_____

_____

Category: 3B (Low Apathy)

Evidence observed that the teacher . . .

Fosters both student and teacher interest in teaching and learning:

_____

_____

_____

_____

Arouses student curiosity and explains the purpose and practical application of content:

_____

_____

_____

_____

Promotes student interest in what goes on in class:

_____

_____

_____

_____

Evidence expected, but not seen:

_____

_____

_____

_____

Category: 3C (Productive Learning Environments)

Evidence observed that the teacher . . .

Maintains a safe and orderly classroom:

_____

_____

_____

_____

Balances established routines and rituals with excitement:

_____

_____

_____

_____

Establishes a physically inviting classroom:

_____

_____

_____

_____

Understands that the classroom climate reflects elements of both the community and school:

_____

_____

_____

_____

Evidence expected, but not seen:

_____

_____

_____

_____

Goals Moving Forward		
Strategy/Activity	**Expected Impact**	**Start & End Dates**
(*Example:* Teams will review learning style inventories and use results to implement research-based instructional strategies that address the learning style preferences of black students.)	(*Example:* December 2011 walkthrough data will show average increases in use of strategies that address the learning style preferences of black students from 29 percent to 59 percent.)	(*Example:* 5/31/11–12/16/11)

WALKTHROUGH FEEDBACK FORM #4:
Classroom Management

Date: _____   Teacher: _____

Grade Level: _____   Subject: _____

Evidence observed that the teacher . . .

Uses appropriate language:

_____

_____

_____

_____

Disciplines using an adult voice:

_____

_____

_____

_____

Tempers order and established standards with equal parts respect—is caring, yet firm:

_____

_____

_____

_____

Prevents situations where students lose peer respect:

_____

_____

_____

_____

Responds to misbehavior on an individual basis:

_____

_____

_____

_____

Matches discipline to students' home culture and language:

_____

_____

_____

_____

Provides explicit coaching on appropriate behavior:

_____

_____

_____

_____

Explicitly communicates expectations of students' roles and behaviors:

_____

_____

_____

_____

Teaches mediation and coping skills:

_____

_____

_____

_____

Evidence expected, but not seen:

_____

_____

_____

_____

Goals Moving Forward		
Strategy/Activity	**Expected Impact**	**Start & End Dates**
(*Example:* Teams will review learning style inventories and use results to implement research-based instructional strategies that address the learning style preferences of black students.)	(*Example:* December 2011 walkthrough data will show average increases in use of strategies that address the learning style preferences of black students from 29 percent to 59 percent.)	(*Example:* 5/31/11–12/16/11)

WALKTHROUGH FEEDBACK FORM #5:
Curriculum and Instructional Design

Date: _____   Teacher: _____

Grade Level: _____   Subject: _____

Category: 5A (Alignment of Goals, Standards, Instruction, and Assessment)

Evidence observed that the teacher . . .

Develops clear goals and standards:

_____
_____
_____
_____

Designs instruction aligned to curriculum content and authentic assessment methods:

_____
_____
_____
_____

Aligns assessments to the content, format, and complexity or level of difficulty of teaching and learning activities:

_____
_____
_____
_____

Evidence expected, but not seen:

_____

_____

_____

_____

Category: 5B (Careful Instructional Planning)

Evidence observed that the teacher . . .

Carefully plans and clearly structures day and lesson content:

_____

_____

_____

_____

Structures lessons to include review of mastered material:

_____

_____

_____

_____

Uses varied systematic strategies for direct reading instruction, such as using encoding principles and maintaining an upbeat climate:

_____

_____

_____

_____

Evidence expected, but not seen:

_____

_____

_____

_____

Category: 5C (Planning for Student Engagement)

Evidence observed that the teacher . . .

Carefully plans the day and lessons to include active engagement:

_____

_____

_____

_____

Designs structured classes and daily routines:

_____

_____

_____

_____

Has and states specific and explicit activity objectives:

_____

_____

_____

Balances facilitation of student learning with teacher-centered presentations to the whole class:

_____

_____

_____

_____

Helps arouse student curiosity by helping students understand the purpose of learning content:

_____

_____

_____

_____

Evidence expected, but not seen:

_____

_____

_____

_____

Category: 5D (Personalized Instruction)

Evidence observed that the teacher . . .

Plans activities to meet the individual developmental needs of diverse students:

_____

_____

_____

_____

Allows students to share in lesson planning:

_____

_____

_____

_____

Evidence expected, but not seen:

_____

_____

_____

_____

Category: 5E (Planning for Cooperative Group Instruction)

Evidence observed that the teacher . . .

Structures environments for cooperative learning and group activities:

_____

_____

_____

_____

Structures group tasks to ensure that students share important roles and develop expertise:

_____

_____

_____

_____

Structures group composition to balance familiar and unfamiliar group members:

_____

_____

_____

_____

Ensures that group goals are attainable:

_____

_____

_____

_____

Evidence expected, but not seen:

_____

_____

_____

_____

Goals Moving Forward		
Strategy/Activity	**Expected Impact**	**Start & End Dates**
(*Example:* Teams will review learning style inventories and use results to implement research-based instructional strategies that address the learning style preferences of black students.)	(*Example:* December 2011 walkthrough data will show average increases in use of strategies that address the learning style preferences of black students from 29 percent to 59 percent.)	(*Example:* 5/31/11–12/16/11)

WALKTHROUGH FEEDBACK FORM #6:
Classroom-Based Assessment

Date: _____   Teacher: _____

Grade Level: _____   Subject: _____

Evidence observed that the teacher . . .

Aligns instruction and curriculum content to authentic assessment methods:

_____

_____

_____

_____

Aligns assessments to the content, format, and complexity or level of difficulty of teaching and learning activities:

_____

_____

_____

_____

Uses frequent continuous assessments to determine skills and knowledge, provides feedback on goals attainment, and creates interventions:

_____

_____

_____

_____

Augments standardized tests with a variety of assessment strategies appropriate to diverse learners, including observations, oral examinations, and performances:

_____

_____

_____

_____

Makes decisions using multiple samples of students' best efforts toward meeting standards, consistently scored against public criteria:

_____

_____

_____

_____

Teaches students how to self-assess and monitor development of skills, knowledge, and dispositions:

_____

_____

_____

_____

Uses culturally sensitive, fair, and unbiased assessments of cognitive and social skills:

_____

_____

_____

_____

Matches assessment to students' language and home culture:

_____

_____

_____

_____

Ensures that language abilities and special needs do not interfere with demonstration of competence by providing coaching, accommodations, and translation support as needed:

_____

_____

_____

_____

Varies content, time, and format of assessment sessions in response to students' energy levels and engagement patterns:

_____

_____

_____

_____

Evidence expected, but not seen:

_____

_____

_____

_____

Goals Moving Forward		
Strategy/Activity	**Expected Impact**	**Start & End Dates**
(*Example:* Teams will review learning style inventories and use results to implement research-based instructional strategies that address the learning style preferences of black students.) _____ _____ _____ _____ _____ _____ _____	(*Example:* December 2011 walkthrough data will show average increases in use of strategies that address the learning style preferences of black students from 29 percent to 59 percent.) _____ _____ _____ _____ _____ _____ _____	(*Example:* 5/31/11–12/16/11) _____ _____

WALKTHROUGH FEEDBACK FORM #7:
Cultural Competence

Date: _____   Teacher: _____

Grade Level: _____   Subject: _____

Category: 7A (Cultural Understanding and Awareness)

Evidence observed that the teacher . . .

Understands how race, ethnicity, language, socioeconomic status, gender, history, residential status, and cultural experience influence behavior, performance, and climate:

_____

_____

_____

_____

Demonstrates knowledge of the modal beliefs, personalities, and interaction, communication, and linguistic styles of varied cultural groups:

_____

_____

_____

_____

Understands cultural variations and nuances of communication related to verbal and nonverbal cues such as gestures, timing, walking, eye glances, dress, and presentation style:

_____

_____

_____

_____

Demonstrates knowledge of the diversity of cultural, ethnic, linguistic, and gender groups in the classroom:

_____

_____

_____

_____

Demonstrates knowledge of students' backgrounds:

_____

_____

_____

_____

Understands the effect of cultural experience on how students construct knowledge:

_____

_____

_____

_____

Understands the effect of racism on students:

_____

_____

_____

_____

Understands aspects of his/her own culture that facilitate or hinder communication with his/her own and other cultural groups:

_____

_____

_____

_____

Evidence expected, but not seen:

_____

_____

_____

_____

Category: 7B (Sensitivity to and Valuing of Cultural Difference)

Evidence observed that the teacher . . .

Communicates validation and acceptance of cultural and gender differences to students:

_____

_____

_____

_____

Shows genuine respect for cultural pride and diversity:

_____

_____

_____

_____

Fosters students' ability to function in their culture of origin:

_____

_____

_____

_____

Evidence expected, but not seen:

_____

_____

_____

_____

Category: 7C (Information in Curriculum on Cultural Differences)

Evidence observed that the teacher . . .

Uses curriculum materials that describe historical, social, and political events from a wide range of racial, ethnic, cultural, and language perspectives:

_____

_____

_____

_____

Investigates topics related to ethnicity, gender, and exceptionality from a wide range of racial, ethnic, cultural, and language perspectives:

_____

_____

_____

_____

Helps each student understand his or her personal perspective, or "self," as one of many cultural perspectives:

_____

_____

_____

_____

Provides curriculum materials on social, economic, and political issues related to ethnicity, gender, and exceptionality:

_____

_____

_____

_____

Helps students understand how personal and cultural experiences influence how they and others construct knowledge:

_____

_____

_____

_____

Provides factual information to refute misconceptions and prejudices about ethnic group members:

_____

_____

_____

_____

Understands and uses information about students' families, cultures, and communities to connect to learning activities:

_____

_____

_____

_____

Encourages mutual sharing of personal and expressive stories related to content:

_____

_____

_____

_____

Evidence expected, but not seen:

_____

_____

_____

_____

Category: 7D (Cultural Critique and Activism)

Evidence observed that the teacher . . .

Helps students understand, critique, and change social structures and practices that produce inequities:

_____

_____

_____

_____

Provides opportunities for students to critique concepts learned, their origins, and their authors' economic, political, and social perspectives and motivations:

_____

_____

_____

_____

Is involved in political struggles aimed at achieving a more just and humane society:

_____

_____

_____

_____

Urges collective action grounded in cultural understanding, experiences, and ways of knowing the world:

_____

_____

_____

_____

Helps students learn how to change elements of society held up to critique:

_____

_____

_____

_____

Provides students with experiences making decisions and taking action about real-world problems:

_____

_____

_____

_____

Evidence expected, but not seen:

_____

_____

_____

_____

Goals Moving Forward		
Strategy/Activity	**Expected Impact**	**Start & End Dates**
(*Example:* Teams will review learning style inventories and use results to implement research-based instructional strategies that address the learning style preferences of black students.) _____ _____ _____ _____ _____ _____ _____	(*Example:* December 2011 walkthrough data will show average increases in use of strategies that address the learning style preferences of black students from 29 percent to 59 percent.) _____ _____ _____ _____ _____ _____ _____	(*Example:* 5/31/11–12/16/11) _____ _____

WALKTHROUGH FEEDBACK FORM #8:
Cultural Congruence in Instruction

Date: _____   Teacher: _____

Grade Level: _____   Subject: _____

Category: 8A (Meaningful, Complex Instruction)

Evidence observed that the teacher . . .

Uses constructivist approaches with student knowledge as the basis for inquiring, representing ideas, developing meaning, elaborating, organizing, and interacting with content:

_____

_____

_____

_____

Teaches a continuum of basic to higher-order literacy skills, knowledge, and ways of thinking to help students derive and convey meaning from text and speech, solve problems, achieve goals, develop individual knowledge and potential, and participate in society:

_____

_____

_____

_____

Develops metacognitive skills that help children learn how to learn:

_____

_____

_____

_____

Provides large amounts of time reading a great variety of texts:

_____

_____

_____

_____

Engages in collaborative team teaching:

_____

_____

_____

_____

Engages all students using meaningful, relevant, and challenging curriculum, content, and instructional activities:

_____

_____

_____

_____

Teaches concepts and skills using integrated, holistic, interdisciplinary lessons:

_____

_____

_____

_____

Engages students in real-life, project-based contextual and vocational activities:

_____

_____

_____

_____

Teaches skills within the context of meaningful applications:

_____

_____

_____

_____

Evidence expected, but not seen:

_____

_____

_____

_____

Category: 8B (Scaffolding Instruction to Home Culture and Language)

Evidence observed that the teacher . . .

Teaches to historical, cultural, social, ethnic, and linguistic differences:

_____

_____

_____

_____

Provides scaffolding to match or link curriculum, materials, lesson content and format, and instructional methods to students' home culture, interests, experiences, and prior learning:

_____

_____

_____

_____

Scaffolds and engages students' learning using visual images and familiar vocabulary to connect prior knowledge and new learning:

_____

_____

_____

_____

Provides core instruction in Standard English:

_____

_____

_____

_____

Teaches academic content in preschool:

_____

_____

_____

_____

Evidence expected, but not seen:

_____

_____

_____

_____

Category: 8C (Responding to Student Traits and Needs)

Evidence observed that the teacher . . .

Demonstrates knowledge of content:

_____

_____

_____

_____

Understands and uses speech and expressions familiar to students:

_____

_____

_____

_____

Selects and uses a variety of instructional methods and interactive strategies:

_____

_____

_____

_____

Varies strategies to meet student's motivational preferences:

_____

_____

_____

_____

Matches instructional strategies to student traits, abilities, and learning style preferences:

_____

_____

_____

_____

Promotes student use of multiple intelligences to gain, use, and respond to knowledge:

_____

_____

_____

_____

Provides materials and learning centers for varied styles and modalities:

_____

_____

_____

_____

Allows students to express visual, tactile, emotional, and auditory preferences:

_____

_____

_____

_____

Incorporates student preferences for verbal expressiveness:

_____

_____

_____

_____

Incorporates student preferences for active kinesthetic participation:

_____

_____

_____

_____

Limits lectures to 5–10 minutes and augments them with visuals and examples:

_____

_____

_____

_____

Evidence expected, but not seen:

_____

_____

_____

_____

Category: 8D (Culturally Relevant Curriculum and Materials)

Evidence observed that the teacher . . .

Selects and uses culturally relevant curriculum materials from and containing all cultural groups:

_____

_____

_____

_____

Selects and uses culturally relevant visual representations of all cultural groups:

_____

_____

_____

_____

Selects and uses culturally relevant books, pictures, and bulletin board items:

_____

_____

_____

_____

Recognizes culturally relevant events:

_____

_____

_____

_____

Uses manipulatives, models, artifacts, and concrete representations of concepts:

_____

_____

_____

_____

Uses primary (original) source materials:

_____

_____

_____

_____

Evidence expected, but not seen:

_____

_____

_____

_____

Goals Moving Forward		
Strategy/Activity	**Expected Impact**	**Start & End Dates**
(*Example:* Teams will review learning style inventories and use results to implement research-based instructional strategies that address the learning style preferences of black students.) _____ _____ _____ _____ _____ _____ _____	(*Example:* December 2011 walkthrough data will show average increases in use of strategies that address the learning style preferences of black students from 29 percent to 59 percent.) _____ _____ _____ _____ _____ _____ _____	(*Example:* 5/31/11–12/16/11) _____ _____

WALKTHROUGH FEEDBACK FORM #9:
Cooperative Group Instruction

Date: _____   Teacher: _____

Grade Level: _____   Subject: _____

Category: 9A (Group Environment and Composition)

Evidence observed that the teacher . . .

Structures environments to allow for cooperative learning and group activities:

_____

_____

_____

_____

Creates flexible student groupings:

_____

_____

_____

_____

Balances familiar and unfamiliar group members when structuring groups:

_____

_____

_____

_____

Creates low-high mixed dyads to enhance achievement for students:

_____

_____

_____

_____

Regularly places students in groups mixed by race, gender, and ability:

_____

_____

_____

_____

Balances facilitated student learning with teacher-centered whole-class presentations:

_____

_____

_____

_____

Evidence expected, but not seen:

_____

_____

_____

_____

Category: 9B (Student Collaboration and Efficacy Development)

Evidence observed that the teacher . . .

Promotes a group-centered collaborative approach toward learning:

_____

_____

_____

_____

Honors students' preference for cohesive group participation when formatting lessons:

_____

_____

_____

_____

Promotes student-to-student assistance for most learning tasks:

_____

_____

_____

_____

Uses a variety of oral and written communication patterns, including pair, team, and whole-class responses following collaborative work:

_____

_____

_____

_____

Ensures that tasks are doable and group goals are attainable:

_____

_____

_____

_____

Ensures that students understand individual roles in content mastery and task completion:

_____

_____

_____

_____

Ensures that all students in groups share important roles and demonstrate their expertise during small-group tasks:

_____

_____

_____

_____

Scaffolds learning and gradually transfers responsibility to students, teaching students to self-monitor skills and knowledge development:

_____

_____

_____

_____

Provides scaffolding through reciprocal teaching in which students gradually assume the role of teacher, helping their peers with learning tasks:

_____

_____

_____

_____

Provides instruction and practice in comprehension strategies such as predicting, generating questions, clarifying, and summarizing using authentic texts:

_____

_____

_____

_____

Evidence expected, but not seen:

_____

_____

_____

_____

Goals Moving Forward		
Strategy/Activity	**Expected Impact**	**Start & End Dates**
(*Example:* Teams will review learning style inventories and use results to implement research-based instructional strategies that address the learning style preferences of black students.)	(*Example:* December 2011 walkthrough data will show average increases in use of strategies that address the learning style preferences of black students from 29 percent to 59 percent.)	(*Example:* 5/31/11–12/16/11)

WALKTHROUGH FEEDBACK FORM #10:
Procedures for Rehearsal, Processing, and Transfer of Learning

Date: _____   Teacher: _____

Grade Level: _____   Subject: _____

Category: 10A (Presenting Information and Ideas)

Evidence observed that the teacher . . .

Uses a variety of modes of representing information and ideas:

_____

_____

_____

_____

Uses global (big-picture) as well as analytical (step-by-step) organizers to describe tasks, including graphic organizers and advance organizers; overviews, lesson outlines, and summarization guides; mnemonics and semantic mapping; and examples and analogies to concretize abstract ideas:

_____

_____

_____

_____

Evidence expected, but not seen:

_____

_____

_____

_____

Category: 10B (Scaffolding between Prior Knowledge and New Learning)

Evidence observed that the teacher . . .

Provides modeling and cognitive scaffolding between prior knowledge and new learning:

_____

_____

_____

_____

Connects new learning to students' prior knowledge using cultural metaphors, personal and relevant examples, multiple concrete representations, and explanations and models:

_____

_____

_____

_____

Evidence expected, but not seen:

_____

_____

_____

_____

Category: 10C (Processing New Content)

Evidence observed that the teacher . . .

Helps students process and internalize information presented:

_____

_____

_____

_____

Creates tools to help students understand information from readings, multimedia resources, site visits, and guests:

_____

_____

_____

_____

Provides modeling and guided practice prior to student demonstrations and tests:

_____

_____

_____

_____

Uses procedures for elaboration of new concepts:

_____

_____

_____

_____

Uses culturally responsive strategies such as call and response, inside-outside discussion circle, visual imagery, and storytelling:

_____

_____

_____

_____

Uses accelerated learning techniques with students at all ability and performance levels, including rehearsal, repetition and periodic review, chunking, music as a memory aid, and memory association maps:

_____

_____

_____

_____

Evidence expected, but not seen:

_____

_____

_____

_____

Category: 10D (Maintaining Active Participation and Managing Time Allocations)

Evidence observed that the teacher . . .

Engages students in multiple ways:

_____

_____

_____

_____

Calls on every student regularly:

_____

_____

_____

_____

Frequently calls for extended, substantive oral and written student responses:

_____

_____

_____

_____

Maintains active learning by using questions and recitation and encouraging student-developed questions:

_____

_____

_____

_____

Maintains active participation by randomly calling on students:

_____

_____

_____

_____

Maintains kinesthetic participation:

_____

_____

_____

_____

Actively engages students in tasks a great deal of the time:

_____

_____

_____

_____

Allows students extended learning time as needed:

_____

_____

_____

_____

Evidence expected, but not seen:

_____

_____

_____

_____

Category: 10E (Ensuring Rigor and Appropriate Task Difficulty)

Evidence observed that the teacher . . .

Continually and appropriately challenges students:

_____

_____

_____

_____

Regularly reminds students that learning will be challenging and rigorous:

_____

_____

_____

_____

Uses challenging materials and tasks:

_____

_____

_____

_____

Creates productive learning environments:

_____

_____

_____

_____

Uses current learning materials and technology:

_____

_____

_____

_____

Evidence expected, but not seen:

_____

_____

_____

_____

Goals Moving Forward		
Strategy/Activity	**Expected Impact**	**Start & End Dates**
(*Example:* Teams will review learning style inventories and use results to implement research-based instructional strategies that address the learning style preferences of black students.) _____ _____ _____ _____ _____ _____ _____	(*Example:* December 2011 walkthrough data will show average increases in use of strategies that address the learning style preferences of black students from 29 percent to 59 percent.) _____ _____ _____ _____ _____ _____ _____	(*Example:* 5/31/11–12/16/11) _____ _____

References

Armor, D. J. (1997, Summer). Why the gap between black and white performance in school? Testimony of David James Armor, March 5, 6, & 22, 1996. (The Role of Social Science in School Desegregation Efforts: The St. Louis Example). *Journal of Negro Education, 66*(3), 258.

Arroyo, A. A., Rhoad, R., & Drew, P. (1999, Summer). Meeting diverse student needs in urban schools: Research-based recommendations for school personnel. *Preventing School Failure, 43*(4), 145.

Banks, J. A., Cookson, P., Gay, G., Hawley, W., Irvine, J. J., Nieto, S., Schofield, J. W., & Stephan, W. G. (2000). *Diversity within unity: Essential principles for teaching and learning in a multicultural society.* Seattle, WA: Center for Multicultural Education, College of Education, University of Washington.

Boozer, M., Krueger, A. B., & Wolkon, S. (1992). *Race and school quality since Brown v. Board of Education.* Washington, DC: Brookings Institution. (ERIC Document Reproduction Service No. ED 296 326)

Cole, R. W. (Ed.). (1995). *Educating everybody's children: Diverse strategies for diverse learners: What research and practice say about improving achievement.* Alexandria, VA: ASCD.

Cook, M. D., & Evans, W. N. (2000, October). Families or schools? Explaining the convergence in white and black academic performance. *Journal of Labor Economics, 18*(4), 729.

Costa, A. L., & Garmston, R. J. (1994). *Cognitive coaching: A foundation for renaissance schools.* Norwood, MA: Christopher-Gordon Publishers.

Cummins, J. (1989). *Empowering minority students.* Sacramento, CA: California Association for Bilingual Education.

Delpit, L. D. (2000, October). *Touched by their fire/ blinded by their brilliance: Reinventing the education of African American children.* Paper presented at the Center for Multicultural Education, College of Education, University of Washington, Seattle, WA.

Durodoyle, B., & Hildreth, B. (1995, September). Learning styles and the African American student. *Education, 116*(2), 241.

Eberly College of Arts & Sciences, West Virginia University. (n.d.). *Strategies for teaching science to African American students.* Retrieved August 2, 2010, from http://www.as.wvu.edu/~equity/african.html

Freel, A. (1998, Spring). Achievement in urban schools: What makes the difference. *Education Digest, 64*(1), 17.

Gallego, M. A., Cole, M., & the Laboratory of Comparative Human Cognition. (2001). Classroom cultures and cultures in the classroom. In V. Richardson (Ed.), *Handbook on research on teaching* (4th ed., pp. 951–997). Washington, DC: American Educational Research Association.

Garcia, E. (1991). *Education of linguistically and culturally diverse students: Effective instruction practices.* Santa Cruz, CA: National Center for Research on Cultural Diversity and Second Language Learning.

Gay, G. (2000). *Culturally responsive teaching: Theory, research, and practice.* New York: Teachers College Press.

Glasser, W. (1994). *Choice theory: A new psychology of personal freedom.* New York: HarperCollins.

Gonzales, N. A., Cauce, A. M., Friedman, R. J., & Mason, C. A. (1996, June). Family, peer, and neighborhood influences on academic achievement among African American adolescents: One-year prospective effects. *American Journal of Community Psychology, 24*(3), 365.

Grant, C. A. (1989). Urban Teachers: Their new colleagues and curriculum. *Phi Delta Kappan, 70,* 746–770.

Haberman, M. (1995). Selecting "star" teachers for children and youth in urban poverty. *Phi Delta Kappan, 76*(10), 777–782.

Haycock, K. (1998, Summer). Good teaching matters: How well-qualified teachers can close the gap. *Thinking K–16, 3*(2), 1–2.

Haycock, K. (2008, May). *Improving achievement and closing gaps: Lessons from schools and districts on the performance frontier.* Paper presented at a meeting of the Delaware Valley Minority Student Achievement Consortium, Philadelphia.

Herrnstein, R. J., & Murray, C. (1994). *The bell curve.* New York: Free Press.

Hill, S. (1999). *African American children: Socialization and development in families.* Thousand Oaks, CA: Sage Publications.

Hilliard, A. G. (March, 2004). *Assessment equity in a multicultural society.* Available at New Horizons for Learning, http://www.newhorizons.org/strategies/assess/hilliard.htm

Hollins, E. R. (1982, January/February). The Marva Collins story revisited: Implications for regular classroom instruction. *Journal of Teacher Education, 33*(1), 37–40.

Hollins, E. R., & Spencer, K. (1990). Restructuring schools for cultural inclusion: Changing the schooling process for African-American youngsters. *Journal of Education, 172*(2), 89–100.

Irvine, J. J. & Armento, B. J. (2001). *Culturally responsive teaching: Lesson planning for elementary and middle grades.* New York: McGraw-Hill.

Knapp, M., & Turnbull, B. (1991). *Better schools for children in poverty: Alternatives to conventional wisdom.* Berkeley, CA: McCutchan.

Ladson-Billings, G. (1994). *The dreamkeepers: Successful teachers for African American children.* San Francisco: Jossey-Bass.

Ladson-Billings, G. (1995). Multicultural teacher education: Research, policy, and practices. In J. A. Banks and C. M. Banks (Eds.), *Handbook of research on multicultural education* (pp. 747–759). New York: McMillan.

Ladson-Billings, G. (2000, May). Fighting for our lives. *Journal of Teacher Education, 51*(3), 206.

McWhorter, J. H. (1997, Summer). Wasting energy on the illusion: Six months later. *The Black Scholar, 27*(2), 2.

National Center for Education Statistics. (2007a). *Status and trends in the education of racial and ethnic minorities.* Retrieved June 9, 2010, from http://nces.ed.gov/pubs2007/minoritytrends/tables/table_4a.asp

National Center for Education Statistics. (2007b). *The condition of education 2007: Characteristics of full-time school teachers.* Washington, DC: U.S. Government Printing Office.

Noguera, P. A., & Akom, A. (2000, June). Causes of the racial achievement gap all derive from unequal treatment: Disparities demystified. *The Nation, 270*(22), 29.

North Central Regional Educational Laboratory (NCREL). (1994). *Strategic Teaching and Reading Project guidebook.* Oak Brook, IL: NCREL.

Palmer, P. (1997). *The courage to teach: Exploring the inner landscape of a teacher's life.* San Francisco: Jossey-Bass.

Pasch, M., Sparks-Langer, G., Gardner, T. G., Starko A. J., & Moody, C. D. (1991). *Teaching as decision making: Instructional practices for the successful teacher.* White Plains, NY: Longman Publishing.

Rogers, E. (1995). *Diffusion of innovations* (4th ed.). New York: The Free Press.

Rowan, B., Chiang, F., & Miller, R. (1997, October). Using research on employees' performance to study the effect of teachers on students' achievement. *Sociology of Education, 70*(4), 256.

Sanders, W., & Rivers, J. (1998). *Cumulative and residual effects of teachers on future academic achievement.* Knoxville, TN: University of Tennessee Value-Added Research and Assessment Center.

Sarason, S. B. (1990). *The predictable failure of educational reform: Can we change course before it's too late?* San Francisco: Jossey-Bass.

Shade, B. J., Kelly, C., & Oberg, M. (1997). *Creating culturally responsive classrooms.* Washington, DC: American Psychological Association.

Simmons, T. (1999, December 27). Worlds apart: The racial education gap. *Raleigh News and Observer.*

Singham, M. (1998, September). The canary in the mine: The achievement gap between black and white students. *Phi Delta Kappan, 80*(1), 8.

Sleeter, C. E., & Grant, C. A. (1988). *Making choices for multicultural education: Five approaches to race, class, and gender.* New York: Macmillan Publishing Company.

Spradlin, L. K., Welsh, L. A., & Hinson, S. L. (2000, Summer). Exploring African American academic achievement: Ogbu and Brookover perspectives. *Journal of African American Men, 5*(1), 17.

State of Washington, Office of the Superintendent of Public Instruction. (2008). *Report on personnel by major position and racial/ethnic for school year 2005–2006.* Retrieved June 9, 2010, from http://www.k12.wa.us/DataAdmin/pubdocs/personnel/stateFTEreport2005-2006.pdf

Stronge, J. H. (2002). *Qualities of effective teachers.* Alexandria, VA: ASCD.

Toch, T. (1998, October 5). The curse of low expectations. *U.S. News and World Report,* p. 60.

Wang, M., & Walberg, H. (1991). Teaching and educational effectiveness: Research synthesis and consensus from the field. In K. J. Rehage (Series Ed.) and H. C. Waxman and H. J. Walberg (Vol. Ed.), *Effective teaching: Current research* (pp. 63–80). Berkeley, CA: McCutchan.

Wigfield, A., Galper, A., & Denton, K. (1999, March). Teachers' beliefs about former Head Start and non-Head Start first-grade children's motivation, performance, and future educational prospects. *Journal of Educational Psychology, 91*(1), 98.

Zeichner, K. M. (1996). Educating teachers to close the achievement gap: Issues of pedagogy, knowledge, and teacher preparation. In B. Williams (Ed.), *Closing the achievement gap: A vision for changing beliefs and practices* (pp. 56–77). Alexandria, VA: ASCD.

Ziegler, C. (2006, Fall). Walk-throughs provide stepped up support. *Journal of Staff Development, 27*(4).

Index

access, 22–24
achievement
    culturally-responsive approaches and, 2
    self-efficacy and, 16–17
achievement gaps
    in African Americans, 3
    reasons for, 2
    statistics, 3–4
    strategies for closing, 2
activism, cultural, 94–95
AECRS. *see* Assessment of Culturally Responsive Strategies (AECRS)
affirmations, 38–39
African Americans, achievement gap of, 3
aligned curriculum, 70–71
apathy, low, 50–51, 135
articulated curriculum, 70–71
assessment
    in Assessment of Effective and Culturally Responsive Strategies (AECRS) form, 137
    bias in, 82–84
    continuous, 82
    cultural responsiveness in, 80–81
    in curriculum design, 70–71
    design of, 80–82
    fairness in, 82–84

assessment *(continued)*
    frequent, 82
    multiple samples in, 82
    observational, 81–82
    parents in, 84
    partners, 84–85
    peers in, 84–85
    pre-assessment, 79–80
    sensitivity in, 82–84
    students as partners in, 84
Assessment of Culturally Responsive Strategies (AECRS), 10
Assessment of Effective and Culturally Responsive Strategies (AECRS) form, 133–142
awareness, cultural, 87–89

bias, in assessment, 82–84
Big Box, The (Morrison), 56
Big Four, 20
body language, 47

caring, 36–40
    affirmations and, 38–39
    in Assessment of Effective and Culturally Responsive Strategies (AECRS) form, 134
    beyond classroom, 40

caring *(continued)*
  ethics and, 38–39
  humor and, 38–39
  manifestations of, 37–38
celebrating diversity, 88–89
change processes, TCRC model and, 6–7
classroom. *see* climate, classroom; management, classroom
climate, classroom
  apathy and, 50–51
  in Assessment of Effective and Culturally Responsive Strategies (AECRS) form, 134–135
  cohesiveness and, 46–50
  exciting, 53–54
  familial, 46–47
  home-school discontinuity and, 48–49
  inviting, 54
  orderly, 52–53
  parent collaboration and, 47–50
  positive, 46–47
  productive learning environments and, 51–54
  responsibility and, 49–50
  safe, 52–53, 54
  structures and, 50
cohesiveness, classroom climate and, 46–50, 134
collaboration, parent, 47–50
commitment, self-efficacy and, 18–19
communication, with parents, 48
comparison, in TCRC model, 8–9
competence, cultural
  activism and, 94–95
  in Assessment of Effective and Culturally Responsive Strategies (AECRS) form, 137–138
  celebration of diversity and, 88–89
  critique and, 94–95
  cultural styles and, 91–92
  curriculum and, 93–94
  as journey, 92–93
  self-awareness and, 91
  sensitivity to difference in, 90–93
  student background knowledge in, 89
  understanding and awareness in, 87–89
  valuing of difference in, 90–93
confidence
  self-efficacy and, 17–18
  sharing, 18
consistency, in expectations, 57–58
constructivist approaches, 98

content knowledge, demonstration of teacher, 103–104
continuous assessment, 82
cooperative group instruction, 74–76. *see also* group instruction
Courage to Teach, The (Palmer), 36
critique, cultural, 94–95
cultural activism, 94–95
cultural awareness, 87–89
cultural critique, 94–95
culturally-responsive approaches
  achievement and, 2
  in assessment design, 80–81
  to discipline, 58–59
  overview of, 5–6
cultural relevance, 106–107
cultural scaffolding, 102–103
cultural style, 91–92
cultural understanding, 87–89
curiosity, student, 73
current materials, 124
curriculum
  aligned, 70–71
  articulated, 70–71
  in Assessment of Effective and Culturally Responsive Strategies (AECRS) form, 136
  careful planning of, 71–72
  challenging, 107
  cultural differences in, 93–94
  cultural relevance in, 106–107
  engagement and, 72–74
  equitable access and, 74
  explicit objectives in, 73
  full inclusion and, 74
  goals in, 70–71
  group instruction planning and, 74–76
  individual approaches in, 71, 74
  meaningful, 107
  personalized instruction and, 72–74
  project-based, 107
  self-efficacy and, 25–26
  standards and, 70–71
  student curiosity and, 73

debrief
  end-of-day, 13–14
  first classroom, 12–13
demographics, of PTP educators, 4–5
demonstrating teacher skill, 103–104

difference, sensitivity to and valuing of, 90–93
discipline
    matching to home culture and language, 58–59
    self-efficacy and, 59
discontinuity, home-school, 48–49
diversity, celebration of, 88–89

Early Scholars Opportunity Program (ESOP), 23
educators. *see* Proving the Possible (PTP) educators
end-of-day debriefing, 13–14
energy, focused, self-efficacy and, 17–18
engagement, curriculum and, 72–74
enjoyment, self-efficacy and, 18–19
environment
    for group instruction, 114
    productive learning, 51–54, 135
equitable access, 22–24, 74
ESOP. *see* Early Scholars Opportunity Program
    (ESOP)
ethics, caring and, 38–39
excitement, balancing routine with, 53–54
expectations
    in Assessment of Effective and Culturally
        Responsive Strategies (AECRS) form, 133
    in classroom management, 57–58
    consistency in, 57–58
    mastery, 21–22
    responsiveness of, 57–58
    role, 21–22
    self-efficacy and, 16–17, 18
    sharing, 18
    standards and, 21–22
    transparency in, 57–58
experiences, sharing personal, 39–40
expertise, in TCRC model, 9
exploration, in TCRC model, 7–8

fairness, 40–43, 134
familial climate, 46–47
family knowledge, of students, 49
favoritism, low, 40–43, 134
focus area, in walkthrough, 10–11
focused energy, self-efficacy and, 17–18
frequent assessment, 82
friction, low, 43, 134
full inclusion, 74

Gardner, Howard, 20
goals, in curriculum design, 70–71

group instruction
    in Assessment of Effective and Culturally
        Responsive Strategies (AECRS) form, 136, 140
    collaboration development in, 114–116
    composition, 114
    cooperative, 74–76
    efficacy development in, 114–116
    environment, 114
    example, 116–120
    preferences in, 115

hard work, self-efficacy and, 18–19
higher order thinking skills, 98–99
Hilliard, Asa, 78
home-school discontinuity, 48–49
humor, 38–39

idea presentation, 122–123
inclusion, full, 74
individual developmental needs, 74
information presentation, 122–123
innovation, self-efficacy and, 19–20
interview, student, in walkthrough, 12
Iowa Test of Basic Skills (ITBS), 5, 18
ITBS. *see* Iowa Test of Basic Skills (ITBS)

kinesthetic engagement, 105–106

language(s)
    discipline matching to home, 58–59
    scaffolding to, 102–103
    in Seattle Public Schools, 4
learning environment, productive, 51–54
learning styles, 104–106
literacy skills development, 99–102
low apathy, 50–51, 135
low favoritism, 40–43, 134
low friction, 43, 134

management, classroom
    in Assessment of Effective and Culturally
        Responsive Strategies (AECRS) form, 135
    discipline matching to home culture and lan-
        guage, 58–59
    example of, 61–68
    expectation setting in, 57–58
    importance of, 55–56
    self-efficacy and, 59
mastery expectations, 21–22

meeting, pre-observation, 11–12
methodology, study, 5
modeling, promoting student interactions through, 42
Montessori program, 25–26
Morrison, Toni, 56
motivation, self-efficacy and, 16–17
music, 105–106

NAEP. *see* National Assessment of Educational Progress (NAEP)
National Assessment of Educational Progress (NAEP), 3
National Urban Alliance (NUA), 53, 71–72, 99, 102, 123
NCE. *see* Normal Curve Equivalent (NCE)
NCLB. *see* No Child Left Behind (NCLB)
new content processing, 123–124
No Child Left Behind (NCLB), 78, 79
Normal Curve Equivalent (NCE), 5
NUA. *see* National Urban Alliance (NUA)

objectives, explicit, 73
observation, in TCRC model, 8
observational assessments, 81–82
opportunities, access to, 22–24
orderly classrooms, 52–53

Palmer, Parker, 36
parents
    as assessment partners, 84
    collaboration with, 47–50
    communication with, 48
    open relations with, 49
    sharing expectations and confidence with, 18
partners, assessment, 84–85
peers, in assessment, 84–85
perceptions, self-efficacy and, 19–20
personal experiences, sharing, 39–40
personalized instruction, 72–74, 136
PISA. *see* Programme for International Student Assessment (PISA)
positive climate, 46–47
practice, in TCRC model, 9
pre-assessment, 79–80
preferences
    honoring, 115
    responding to, 105–106
pre-observation preparation meeting, 11–12

presentations, teacher-centered, 73
presenting information and ideas, 122–123
processing new content, 123–124
productive learning environments, 51–54, 135
professional development
    self-awareness through, 91
    self-efficacy and, 20–21
Programme for International Student Assessment (PISA), 3
project-based learning, 107
Proving the Possible (PTP) educators
    caring by, 36–40
    demographics of, 4–5
    demonstrating content knowledge and skills by, 103–104
    diversity of, 1–3
    ethnic makeup of, 4
    experience levels of, 4
    investment of, 3
    personal experience sharing by, 39–40
    student background knowledge by, 89
PTP. *see* Proving the Possible (PTP) educators
purposeful instruction, 42–43

reading, NAEP scores, 3–4
Read Naturally program, 23, 26
reflection, in TCRC model, 8
relationships, beyond classroom, 40
relevance, cultural, 106–107
resources, access to, 22–24
respect, 40–43, 134
responsibility
    classroom climate and, 49–50
    fostering, 24–27
    shared, 26–27
responsiveness, in expectations, 57–58
rituals
    balancing with excitement, 53–54
    for safe and orderly classrooms, 52–53
role expectations, 21–22
role sharing, in group work, 75–76
routines
    balancing with excitement, 53–54
    for safe and orderly classrooms, 52–53

safety, classroom, 52–53, 54
Sarason, Seymour B., 5
SAT. *see* Scholastic Aptitude Test (SAT)
scaffolding to culture and language, 102–103

Scholastic Aptitude Test (SAT), 3
Seattle Public Schools, 4
self-awareness, in professional learning, 91
self-efficacy
    achievement and, 16–17
    classroom management and, 59
    commitment and, 18–19
    confidence and, 17–18
    curriculum and, 25–26
    enjoyment and, 18–19
    expectations and, 16–17, 18
    focused energy and, 17–18
    fostering, 24–27
    hard work and, 18–19
    innovation and, 19–20
    motivation and, 16–17
    perceptions and, 19–20
    professional development and, 20–21
sensitivity
    in assessment, 82–84
    to differences, 90–93
shared responsibility, with teachers and students, 26–27
sharing expertise, 9
sharing personal experiences, 39–40
sharing roles, in group instruction, 75–76
standards
    in curriculum design, 70–71
    expectations and, 21–22
statistics, achievement gap, 3–4
student assessment partners, 84–85
student background, teacher knowledge of, 89
student curiosity, 73
student favoritism, 40–43
student interactions, promotion of, 42–43
student interview walkthrough, 12
student responsibility
    fostering, 24–27
    shared, 26–27
student voices, in TCRC model, 9
study methodology, 5
style
    cultural, 91–92
    learning, 104–106
support, beyond classroom, 40

Synonym Triplets, 101–102

TCRC. *see* Teaming for Culturally Responsive Classrooms (TCRC) model
teachers. *see* Proving the Possible (PTP) educators
Teaming for Culturally Responsive Classrooms (TCRC) model
    change processes and, 6–7
    comparison in, 8–9
    expertise in, 9
    exploration in, 7–8
    overview of, 5–6
    phases of, 7–9
    reflection in, 8
    student voices in, 9
    teamwork and, 6–7
    walkthrough protocol, 9–14
teams, walkthrough, 11
teamwork, TCRC model and, 6–7
technology, 124
training, of walkthrough teams, 11
transparency, in expectations, 57–58

understanding, cultural, 87–89

valuing differences, 90–93
verbal expressiveness, 105–106

walkthrough protocol, 9–14
    conduction of, 12
    end-of-day debrief in, 13
    example of, 27–34
    first classroom debrief in, 12–13
    focus area selection in, 10–11
    pre-observation preparation meeting in, 11–12
    student interview in, 12
    teams in, 11
"warm demanders," 40
Washington Assessment of Student Learning (WASL), 5, 39, 78
WASL. *see* Washington Assessment of Student Learning (WASL)
Word Market, 102
Word Snatch, 106
Word Wall, 102, 106

About the Author

Johnnie McKinley is passionate about helping implement two changes that are proven to improve achievement for all students, particularly students of color: changing teacher-student classroom interactions and engaging parents and the community as knowledgeable advocates for children. She has been invested in teacher development as coordinator for district-level professional development, teacher certification, and induction programs, and has served as a district-level director of equity and achievement. She has more than 25 years experience in organizational development, training, conference presentation, marketing, and program evaluation.

Dr. McKinley earned her Ed.D. in educational leadership with a cognate in business administration from Seattle University, and has served as adjunct professor in educational psychology at the College of Education at the University of Washington in Seattle for a number of years. Dr. McKinley travels the United States as a presenter and consultant on organizational change, school reform, school safety, bias and fairness in assessments, and donor research and grant writing. She has presented her research findings regarding the PTP teachers discussed in this book at over 60 national and international conferences. In 2005, she was nominated for the American Educational Research Association and National Staff Development Council Dissertation awards.